Still Life
with Brook
Trout

☙

John Gierach

Illustrated by Glen Wolff

Simon & Schuster Paperbacks

New York   London   Toronto   Sydney

SIMON & SCHUSTER PAPERBACKS
Rockefeller Center
1230 Avenue of the Americas
New York, NY 10020

First Simon & Schuster paperback edition 2006

Portions of this book in different form first appeared in Field & Stream, Fly Rod & Reel, The Longmont Daily Times-Call and Sports Afield.

SIMON & SCHUSTER PAPERBACKS and colophon are registered trademarks of Simon & Schuster, Inc.

For information about special discounts for bulk purchases, please contact Simon & Schuster Special Sales at 1-800-456-6798 or business@simonandschuster.com

Designed by Karolina Harris

Illustrations copyright Glen Wolff

Manufactured in the United States of America

1 3 5 7 9 10 8 6 4 2

Library of Congress Cataloging-in-Publication Data

Gierach, John, date.
Still life with brook trout / John Gierach.
p. cm.
1. Fishing—Anecdotes. 2. Gierach, John, date. I. Title.
SH441.G524 2005
799.17'57—dc22   2004056614
ISBN-13: 978-0-7432-2994-4
ISBN-10:   0-7432-2994-0
ISBN-13: 978-0-7432-2995-1 (Pbk)
ISBN-10:   0-7432-2995-9 (Pbk)

We should be grateful for impermanence and the freedom it grants us.

GARY SNYDER

STILL LIFE
with BROOK
TROUT

Chapter 1

VINCE ZOUNEK and I had pulled off the road on a wooded pass for one of those stops that are made necessary by a long drive and too much coffee. This was an ideal spot to pee. You could easily get out of sight of the road to avoid offending anyone who drove by, and to the east there was a fine view of receding peaks, the farther mountains still purple in the cloudy morning light. We'd stopped at this same pretty spot plenty of times on previous trips up this road, but apparently not often enough to kill the grass.

As we walked back toward his pickup, Vince said "Uh oh" in the kind of noncommittal tone of voice that could have meant anything from an untied shoelace to a charging bull. Turns out he was referring to the steaming green pool of radiator fluid that was growing under the front bumper of his truck.

I've always enjoyed being on the road—even at times like

this—because the usual complications of life suddenly boil down to simply getting where you're going; in this case, to a little trout stream in Wyoming that we'd never fished before. The big uncertain future you're always worrying about shrinks to the time it takes to get to the creek, and then unexpectedly shrinks again to the distance between a mountain pass and the nearest radiator shop, which we guessed at about twenty miles. Most of that distance was downhill, but while the temperature gauge wasn't quite pegged, it was dangerously high.

Vince said, "What do you think? Can we make it without seizing up?"

I said, "It's your truck, man," trying to be as helpful as possible without accepting any responsibility.

A few miles down the road, the engine temperature had actually cooled slightly and Vince was puzzled by that. I explained that when a vehicle stops, the cooling system shuts down and the temperature climbs from the stored heat of the engine. Once you're moving, the coolant begins to circulate again, and even when there isn't much of it left, it still makes a difference. (I was channeling my late father here. Internal combustion engines are actually one of my weak points.)

Vince enjoyed that. I like traveling with him because he's the kind of guy who can take the time to appreciate an interesting new fact even when the larger picture looks grim. I was smiling over the idea that something my dad told me when I was a kid had popped out forty-some years later sounding like wisdom. The temperature hovered just inside the red as we coasted down off the pass, and for the next few miles we were unreasonably happy.

The guy at the radiator shop in town said it was just a cracked hose; he had the part and could get right to it, so we killed some time drinking coffee and wandering Main Street in the kind of wind that snatches your hat and sandblasts your face. The question about wind in Wyoming isn't, Will it blow? but rather, How hard and from which direction? I've learned that when I cross the Colorado line into Wyoming, I have to ditch the brimmed fishing hat—never mind the sunburned ears—and screw on a baseball cap adjusted one size too small.

When we went to pick up the truck, the man in front of us at the counter had a squirrel sitting on his shoulder, a fat one that had apparently lived a pampered life in captivity. This is the kind of thing that doesn't quite register at first. You have to stop and say to yourself, That man has a live fox squirrel on his shoulder.

The squirrel turned out to be friendly enough in the excitable way of a critter that will never be completely tame— not unlike the human he was with, actually. When I tried to make up to the squirrel, he immediately hopped onto my shoulder and started nuzzling around like we were old friends.

Vince said, "You've always had a way with animals."

I said, "Yeah, but I also have an open bag of peanuts in my jacket."

When the man and his squirrel left, the radiator guy looked after them and said, "No one in that whole family is quite right."

We were on our way again by noon. We'd only gone a few miles out of our way and we'd only lost an hour and a half of fishing time, but it was early in the season when morning fishing isn't that good anyway. Not bad as breakdowns go. All in all, this is how it had been going for the last couple of seasons. Things hadn't been working out perfectly, but they'd been working out.

The stretch of stream we had permission to fish ran across a wide, flat valley of hay meadows bordered by low foothills. A minor range of the Rocky Mountains was just barely visible to the west as a line of uneven gray bumps on the horizon. If you didn't already know it was there, you might not even notice it.

The creek was downstream of a wedge-shaped irrigation dam that split an already small stream into two smaller channels, and at first glance it was hard to tell which was the original watercourse and which was the ditch. We guessed that the right fork was the actual stream because what we could see of it wandered off in wide meanders, while the left fork took a forty-five-degree dogleg and then went straight. Real streams meander because they're in no particular hurry; ditches go straight because they are.

We walked a few hundred yards down that right fork and found distinct pools and riffles, a few still-active spring seeps, and stands of old, gnarled river birch that had gotten plenty of sun and water, but were as stubby and contorted as bonsai trees from living in a constant wind. This had to be it. A quarter mile across the meadow we could see the other channel. It was lined in scrubby willows and it ran as straight as a city street.

The flow in the stream was low for May and in fact, it would have seemed a little low even for August or September. In a normal year, any stream in this country would have been in the early stages of runoff, maybe even too high and muddy to fish, but it had been yet another dry winter, so maybe this was all the snowmelt there was.

But then we'd sort of counted on that. Normally you'd never drive a hundred miles to try out a new stream in May.

You'd go in early April, hoping to slip in before the spring runoff began, or wait until sometime in late June or even early July when it came down. But over the previous two drought seasons the usual timing had slipped a few gears. Now, May could be a good month to fish a new stream. In many drainages up and down the Front Range, the slug of snowmelt that was usually a seasonal flood had been no more than relief from the low flows of winter, and since there was less of it, the water warmed more quickly toward the high 40s: the temperature that starts the aquatic insects moving around and the trout feeding.

Of course in a strange creek half a dozen drainages north of home, it was a guess, but no more of a guess than when the runoff would come up or go down in another kind of year. Still, it was something to go on. One of the charms of fishing is that it's always a gamble, but then one of the charms of gambling is that you can use what you think you know to play the odds. Some make obscene amounts of money doing things like that with stocks, bonds and hog futures. Others just manage to catch a few trout.

The stream was lower than we expected it to be, but we thought we'd still figured it right. We just hadn't counted on that headgate taking a third of its flow to flood-irrigate hay fields. For that matter, there would be other ranches upstream between there and the mountains, each with its own water rights, and they'd probably done the same thing. Once upon a time, creeks and rivers converged and grew as they flowed downstream; now they split and shrink. It's one more example of how things can go sideways when humans are in charge. Somewhere up there above the last ranches and headgates, in the national forest, this creek was probably running a reasonably healthy head of water, the drought notwithstanding.

• • •

The fishing that day turned out to be pretty tough. Most of the stream ran thin and ankle-deep, although the water was still cold and there was still enough of it to make the riffles sound like distant laughter. There were some glassy, slow-moving, fishy-looking pools here and there that would have been a challenge to fish even on a calm day, but the wind was blowing so hard that casting was an additional struggle. This was the kind of situation where you needed a heavy nine-foot, nine-weight rod to make the cast and a delicate little seven-foot, four-weight to fish the fly. If I remember right, we were both fishing five-weights.

At least it was cloudy, which would make the trout a little less spooky, and the wind was ruffling the water enough to cover the less than perfect casts we were making. On a calm, bright day, this would approach being impossible. As it was, this would only be difficult.

In most places, the only way to get a quiet cast and drift was to slam a dry fly and a dropper at the head of a pool against the upstream wind, make a big mend, hold your rod tip low to keep the wind from whipping the line around and then let it slowly snake down into the sweet spot. Sometimes we'd do this from our knees to keep our silhouettes low. Sometimes we'd cast to the current twenty feet above a pool, crawl downstream on our hands and knees behind the slowly floating fly and then lie on our stomachs to fish out the drift. Once you've decided to do serious stealth, you can hardly go too far. There's the temptation to stick twigs in your hat so you look like a bush.

It could take several minutes to fish out a drift in the lazy current and during these almost cinematic slow-motion scenes it was possible to get distracted by a deer crossing a meadow or a circling hawk and miss a strike when it finally came. And in that glassy water, the commotion caused by missing a strike could mean you'd buggered the pool.

We caught a handful of fish that afternoon and they all came hard, but more because of the wind, the agonizing drifts and being asleep at the wheel when the takes came than from any real skittishness on the fishes' part. There was no hatch to speak of, but the creek had warmed up early, so there were a few odd caddis flies, mayflies and crane flies around. These trout wanted a good, natural-looking drift in the right spot, but they hadn't been fished for enough to have gotten too picky about flies. Our first guesses at what the right fly might be worked well enough—and we each picked different patterns.

These were fat, healthy-looking brown trout—butter yellow with brown backs, bottomless black spots and that hint of iridescent sky blue on their gill covers—and some were surprisingly big. I got one that was around sixteen inches long and missed a bigger one when my attention strayed during a five-minute drift and I forgot to set the hook. Vince landed one that he measured against his net handle at a fraction over nineteen inches. These would have been good-sized trout anywhere, but they seemed even bigger coming out of low water in a small creek. We were proud of ourselves. It was more than we'd expected, but, in the way of fishermen everywhere, not exactly more than we'd hoped for.

That had pretty much been our experience as fly fishermen living through the past two years of drought: We'd tried a little harder and done better than we expected—sometimes even better than usual—even though the drought was having undeniably real effects on the streams and rivers in the West.

Summer rains and winter snows had both been way below the thirty-year average they call "normal," and the dry winters had been especially worrisome, since the region gets more than 80 percent of its water from melting snow running out of the high mountains.

Water providers—who make millions selling water and for whom there will never be enough—had been howling about how we needed more dams for storage so we could go on wasting water even in drought conditions. But then they also howl for dams in wet years (for flood control) and in normal years to provide more water for growth. By now this has become little more than a kind of background noise, but they do turn up the volume during extreme conditions when it's easier to incite panic.

Guides and fly-shop owners were worried because business was down, although the more established outfits thought they'd weather the drought okay as long as it didn't go on "forever"—by which they meant another year or two. Some even said that the slow seasons would flush some of the deadwood out of the fishing business, although none of those in danger of getting flushed thought of themselves as "deadwood."

And naturally those fishermen with a tendency toward hysteria were making the usual dire predictions of the end of fishing as we know it. I can't say I was completely unconcerned myself, but in the thirty-five years I've lived in the region I'd seen five multiyear droughts and about that many flood years—enough to begin to see that a normal year was more the exception than the rule. I had also heard many doomsday predictions, none of which quite came to pass.

It's true that some lakes and reservoirs were down and some streams and rivers were running thin, but the catastrophe seemed to be less real and more a matter of definition. That is, there was less water than some people wanted, but there was no less water than there was supposed to be or than there had been off and on for as far back as records had been kept.

The Front Range of the Rockies has a semiarid climate where the air routinely gets dry enough to evaporate the ice cubes in your freezer, and in some places there are already more people than there is water to support them, especially since many insist on growing exotic, water-guzzling trees and lawns. The drought was a problem because we were already asking more from the environment than it was able to give, so the unavoidable question had to be, If the habitat we've chosen to live in is doing what it's always done and we call that a disaster, what does that say about us? The all-too-common answer was, "We don't care what it says, we just wanna water our lawns." Living gracefully in any kind of natural environment takes patience and acceptance: the two qualities we Americans have pretty much bred out of ourselves.

As for the fishing, it had held up well enough so far. Some of the mountain lakes we fished had dropped a little, but they still seemed fine. The untouched streams—those above the last dams and cutoffs—were running at the thin end of normal, but they also seemed fine. In fact, the low runoff had added a month to the beginning of the high-country season and the insect hatches had been starting early and staying late. It was mostly the man-made fisheries—the reservoirs and tailwaters—that were taking the hit, and since those were the most popular places with the biggest trout and the biggest crowds, things looked worse than they were.

In some canyon streams, the drought had actually helped the trout. When spring runoff comes down a steep-sided canyon, the stream doesn't spread out and get wider as it would in flatter country; it just gets deeper and faster, making it harder for the trout to feed and messing up the redds of spring-spawning rainbows and cutthroats. Low runoff lengthens the fishes' growing season and makes life easier for young trout, which can feed more easily in slower currents. According to a Colorado Division of Wildlife study, after two drought years the trout biomass in the Arkansas River had doubled and the number of trout over fourteen inches had increased eightfold.

Rafting companies on the Arkansas were hurting because there wasn't enough high water for their usual paid thrill rides, but fishermen had an extra month of dry-fly fishing and, by all accounts, they didn't miss rafts filled with squealing tourists paddling through the water they were trying to fish. You try not to wish hard times on people who work for a living—if only because ill will can come back to bite you—but in this case it was possible to not lose any sleep over it.

From what I could see, the low runoff was also helping many of the small streams at higher altitudes that were too obscure or too remote to rate their own studies. For every low-altitude creek that was surviving, but a little too thin to fish, there was another higher up that was doing beautifully, with adequate flows and fatter trout. There may have been fewer places to fish than usual, but with news of the drought in the West making national headlines, the crowds of tourist fly fishers had thinned out and even some residents stayed home, preferring to believe the drought coverage in newspapers and on TV instead of going out to see for themselves. That meant that those of us who did go out had more water to ourselves.

Of course it's hard to be completely immune to a media-induced panic (if only because the media orchestrate those so effectively) and there were days when I wondered if I should worry more. But then I naturally went on to wonder what good worrying would do. I was catching fish—which is central to any fisherman's view of reality—and I was even getting pretty adept at casting delicately in slower water. This is the kind of thing we've all learned to live with in recent years: You're on orange alert, but there's nothing you can do about it, so you go about your life—as per the administration's instructions—now and then glancing over your shoulder without knowing what you expect to see. This will probably never seem quite right, but it does feel progressively less insane as time goes by.

We were a good two miles down that creek in Wyoming when we stopped to watch a huge flock of red-winged blackbirds come stalling and skidding in on the wind and land in the upper branches of a grove of river birch. It was late in the day and the birds were coming in to roost, looking like fluttering black leaves sprouting in the still-bare trees and making their usual springtime racket that sounded like two hundred screen doors with rusty hinges about to slam. Redwings are among my dozen or so favorite birds. I've carefully arranged it so that all my favorites are locally common. That way I get to see them often and the world seems friendlier.

We looked at the sky, and then at our watches, and saw that there was enough daylight left to walk back out without running into something in the dark. And there'd been plenty to run into: fallen trees, a dead harrow camouflaged by rust and weeds, snarls of barbed wire hidden in tall grass. There were dozens of accidents waiting to happen to someone who couldn't see what he was doing.

11

On the walk back we decided to add this stream to the dozens of others that we wouldn't worry about just yet. It had held out through some drought years already and would probably continue to hold out unless things got worse. When the little bit of runoff there was flushed out later in the year, the water would drop even more, but by then irrigation season would be over and the headgates would be closed, so although there'd be less water, more of it would stay in the stream. Over the last few years that had apparently been enough to grow and support some big brown trout.

That may have been largely accidental as far as the rancher was concerned, but it had still worked out okay for the fish. And anyway, it's easy to criticize ranchers for siphoning off streams to grow hay, but it gets a little harder when you remember that hay feeds cattle and you eat beef and wear leather, and then it gets harder still when the guy gives you permission to fish and you catch some big ones. When you step back even a little bit to get a slightly larger view, moral clarity is harder to come by and your sense of outrage gets diluted by your own complicity. Things could have been better, but when the trout survive, life can't be all bad.

Back at the truck at dusk, we both stopped to look under the front bumper, but there was no puddle of radiator fluid; not even a little wet spot from slow drip. We had a long drive ahead of us and for the immediate future at least, things looked promising.

Chapter 2

JIM BABB met me at the airport in Bangor, Maine, and asked, as you're supposed to ask to be polite, "How was your flight?"

I said, "The flight was fine, but I must have been randomly profiled in Denver because security was a bitch. For about fifteen minutes I was the prime suspect. At least I wasn't cavity-searched."

The answer to "How was your flight?" can be a lot longer now than it once was. At its worst, it's like saying "How are you?" to a hypochondriac.

Then, as we walked toward an escalator, I asked, "So, how's it look?"

Jim said, "Well, not great."

My heart did not sink. When you travel to fish, you hear that often enough and you're expected to take it like a man, as we used to say. It doesn't always turn out to be true anyway—anything can happen on the water, including the good stuff—

and even when it *is* true, it's still just fishing. It's not like a death sentence or anything.

We rode the escalator down to the baggage carousel and stood around with sixty or seventy other passengers like gamblers around a roulette wheel. We'd all bet that our luggage would arrive when we did. Now we were waiting to see if we were right. There are no guarantees on travel any more than there are on fishing. There are only degrees of likelihood.

The plan was to drive north, meet Paul Guernsey and Dave Gallipoli at a cabin on Frost Pond, and fish a nearby river for landlocked salmon—a fish I'd heard about, but had never caught—but conditions had been weird. There'd been a serious drought in Maine the previous winter—not unlike the one back home in Colorado—except that theirs had been followed by the coldest, rainiest spring since the 1860s. Enough rain fell to more than break their drought—which was good—but it was also enough to swell the rivers and chill the water—which was bad because landlocked-salmon fishing is all about flow and temperature.

Landlocked salmon are just what the name says: Atlantic salmon that are landlocked in fresh water, so that instead of running out to the ocean to grow big on shrimp and herring, they run to deep lakes and get somewhat less large, but still plump, on forage fish like smelt. Aside from that technicality, they're either just like Atlantic salmon or they *are* Atlantic salmon, depending on whom you ask.

By all accounts, a twenty-inch landlock weighing close to three pounds is considered a good one, at the high end of normal and full of fight, and in most places, anything over five pounds could be the fish of a lifetime. At least that's what Dr. Robert Behnke says in his beautiful and authoritative book *Trout and Salmon of North America,* although I've talked to fishermen from the Northeast who claim to regularly catch them up to eight and ten pounds. And they can get bigger. Behnke cites historical reports of landlocks from Lake Ontario weighing over forty pounds, but those would have been amazing fish even back in the good old days, and that population is now said to be extinct.

Landlocks are essentially lake fish (they're also called "lake salmon") but they swim up the rivers to feed in the spring when the water rises and warms. Later they drop back into the lakes to wait out the heat of summer, then run back up the rivers when the water cools in the fall to feed again for a while, and then spawn.

They're not technically anadromous because they don't go to salt water, but the effect on the fishing is the same: You wade into a landlocked salmon river knowing that, in the grand scheme of things, the fish are more likely to be absent than present. We inland fishermen have trouble grasping that. There are plenty of days when we can't catch fish (even though we know they're in there and we might even be able to see one now and then), but the idea that an entire population could be altogether elsewhere is troubling.

But your one advantage with landlocks is that, unlike sea-run Atlantic salmon, they eat while they're in the rivers. You fish for them the way you would for trout: sometimes with streamers, sometimes with whatever dry flies or nymphs seem right at the time. On the long drive north, Jim said, "They're just like Atlantic salmon except they bite for reasons you can understand." He also said, "Fishing for landlocked salmon is like scale-model Atlantic salmon fishing: all the frustration for a fraction of the price."

Fishing for migratory fish is hard enough to predict when

things are more or less as they should be, but when conditions begin to get strange, even those who know what they're doing can be at a loss. Here it was June, when the spring run should have been just past its peak with the river full of fish, but the weather was grayer and colder than it should have been and the rivers were still too high and chilly. Only a few small salmon were in, and even those weren't biting well.

Someone suggested that the salmon either couldn't get up the rapids in the high water, or just didn't want to, or that maybe the water was still too cold, so all but a few were holding back. Any or all of that meant the run would either be late or nonexistent. Someone else thought the drought that past winter had dried up the streams where the shad spawn, and then the high water had "blown out" the remaining baitfish, leaving the salmon without their main food source.

Whatever it was, the fishing had been poor enough that people had moved beyond trying to figure out why and on to why it could continue to be bad all season and possibly for years to come. Fishermen theorize desperately when they're not catching fish, especially when there's a newcomer around. They're trying to be helpful.

My first landlocked salmon was eight or nine inches long and really was a scale model of an Atlantic salmon: streamlined, silvery, shading to bronze on the back, with scattered spots and firm as a bratwurst. It hit hard, jumped and fought ferociously. It did everything a baby fish could do against a seven-weight fly rod. It couldn't do much, but I was still impressed. I could see how if you put another pound or two on that fish, he could rip you a new one.

I learned that in Maine little fish are called "tiddlers." I said, "Back home we just call them 'little fish.'"

It went on like that for a few days. Precious few salmon were caught and the ones we did land were mostly tiddlers. Everyone apologized for the fishing: Jim, Paul, Dave, a guy at a general store, a woman in a fly shop. "It's not usually like this," they said. I told them I understood, although in my experience, fishing for any kind of salmon is *exactly* like this.

We fished steadily and patiently anyway because that's what you do: You methodically go through the motions so you'll be ready if and when it happens. We'd go to a good spot—usually a stretch of slack current above or below some rapids—cast for a while, then sit and rest the spot, then start fishing again. Salmon prowl. If they're not here now, they could be here in half an hour. Or tomorrow. Or next month.

This is where locals have the advantage—the same advantage I have back home. You can go home, try to do something useful, keep your ear to the ground and come back on short notice when things turn around.

As a tourist fisherman with a return plane ticket in your pocket, you suck it up and take your shot and it's amazing how often it works out. You can't expect to hit it dead on with every trip—although that does happen now and then—but there are usually fish and if you pay attention and bear down a little, you usually catch some. And when a trip really does go in the crapper, as one will eventually, you are still somehow fulfilling your destiny as a fisherman, and that's bound to be for the best.

They said that people had fished for landlocked salmon here for 150 years and there were no secrets left. All the good spots were known, including the most comfortable rocks to sit on. But then Jim took me to one of his favorite runs and said, "Never start in here at the same place. That way we won't wear a trail." He'd park his car far enough away to look like we'd gone somewhere else and we'd always make sure no one was coming up or down the dirt road before we stepped off into the woods. We spent a lot of time there and always had it to ourselves. We caught a few smallish salmon and one day I hooked and lost a big brook trout. It was sixteen or seventeen inches long and I had it on just long enough to get a quick look before it spit the hook.

Still, I was deeply happy to be in that country and the long dead spells in the fishing gave me time to look around and take it all in. The woods were thick, cool, humid and wildly diverse. There were five different kinds of birch tree, for instance. There were big-headed, long-necked pileated woodpeckers with 2 1/2-foot wingspans lofting through the woods like pterodactyls. There were miniature clearings filled with blue and pink lupine flowers, and down along the river you'd now and then find a single, small wild iris. (These were the first struggling flowers of a late bloom. According to the phenology of this river, wild irises and salmon come together.) Back at the cabin, loons laughed hysterically out on Frost Pond and at night there were tree frogs that made a noise like squirrels slowly chewing ice.

At the office of the place where we were staying, I met a genuine Maine coon cat, an animal I've always admired. He was a long-haired, twenty-pound bruiser with dog-sized feet and an impassive gaze. It's said that the breed originated when the cats belonging to the early settlers interbred with raccoons. That's not true, of course—in fact, it's impossible—it's just that cold climates favor large animals over small ones, from snowshoe hares to moose. This was just the northwoods, mega-fauna version of a pussycat.

It all reminded me of the boreal forests in Minnesota that I first saw while fishing with my father on family vacations. That was where I got my first real taste for wild country, influenced not only by the lakes, woods and fish, but by the nostalgic calendar art that hung in every cafe and hardware store at the time. You know, those idealized paintings of lean, serious men in plaid shirts and fedoras paddling wooden canoes. I was twelve or thirteen years old then—more innocent than kids are now, but no less eager to lose that innocence— and I naturally imprinted on the north woods the way an orphan gosling will fasten on the first thing it sees move. Northern Maine and northern Minnesota seem the same because they're at opposing ends of the same primordial bioregion, and from the first day in the Maine woods, I had the eerie feeling that sometimes comes to travelers of being cozily at home in a place they've never been before.

A few days into the trip, we decided we'd pounded the local water hard enough and tried another river about a two hours' drive north. Paul kept pointedly referring to it as "The River Whose Name Must Not Be Spoken" and I took the hint so well that I now can't remember its real name. The trip was a shot in the dark because this was a small, short stream connecting two lakes and there were only two good pools on it. If they were already taken—as they might well have been— the long drive would be a bust.

The day was dark and chilly, still dripping from the last rain and threatening more. I didn't ask if that was auspicious or not, but it's the kind of weather I've always associated with good fishing. It was easy to believe that this was, in fact, the wettest year since the Civil War, and I was jealous thinking of the drought back home. I thought, Why couldn't they have a little less and we have a little more? The kind of stupid, but honest question we can't help asking. I also wondered if there might be a midpoint in the nearly two thousand miles between home with too little water and here with too much where things were exactly right. The North Shore of Minnesota, southern Manitoba . . . I tried to make that an idle thought because it's deadly to start thinking you should be somewhere else when, for one reason or another, you can't be.

There was an old muddy logging road along the creek. We met two fishermen coming out as we were going in and everyone bristled harmlessly. This is public land, but every fisherman naturally thinks of the creek as his. When they'd passed out of earshot, someone mumbled that they looked like they were from New Jersey. I glanced at them over my shoulder, but didn't notice anything unusual. It turned out that the two pools Paul wanted were both open, so we spread out and started fishing.

Early on, drifting an Elk Hair Caddis with a soft-hackle dropper, I landed a chubby sixteen-inch salmon that jumped twice and even took a little line. It was a good tussle, lasting a couple of minutes, and there was some excitement all around, but then that was it. Over the next few hours the wind picked up steadily until casting started to get dangerous. The rain came on slowly at first, but when it built to a downpour, we trudged back to the car with the hoods up on our rain slickers and our heads bowed against the wind. A little caddis hatch had been starting to come off, but the rain put an end to it.

On the drive back after dark, we saw five moose in the road. Moose are big, but they're also black, so when they show up in the headlights at all, they're just a darker spot in the general darkness—like a hairy black hole in space—and it's possible to not see one until it's ten feet from your front bumper. I spotted the first one when it was way too close and yelled "Whoa!" Jim hit the brakes and said, "The proper term is *Moose! Whoa!* could mean anything."

I thought we were going a little too fast, given the muddy road and the poor visibility, and since my life could depend on the proper terminology, I started silently chanting, "moose, moose, moose . . ."

The next day, Paul and Dave went back to the River Whose Name Must Not Be Spoken and Jim and I tried a couple of little streams that might have had brook trout in them, but didn't. Apparently brook trout use the streams the same way salmon do: running up into them from the lakes only when things are damned near perfect. A friend back home had said, "I hear there's a lot of downtime to Maine fishing."

I mentioned that to Jim and he said, "Yup."

That night at the cabin, the four of us compared notes, but there wasn't much to report except that Jim and I had puttered around on back roads, talking and fishing casually and picking up the odd salmon parr or fingerling brookie, while Paul and Dave had fished long and hard and looked haggard. If the fish won't show you what they're about, all you have to do is look at the fishermen. The thousand-yard stare says it all and if you're not wearing that expression yourself, it's only because you don't fully grasp the situation.

Then Dave went into the kitchen to rustle up a restaurant-quality Italian meal, and over dinner we laughed about our . . . what? Failure? Well, that's not quite it. We'd planned to go fishing and here we were fishing, so that part had worked out perfectly. I think most of us fish not so much to become one

with nature—which sounds too much like an advertising slo-
gan—but to be skillful at life as it actually is, however it turns
out. I knew I was with the right bunch of guys because how
it had turned out that week finally struck us all as just funny
as hell.

The next day we were on yet another salmon river, figuring
that if the first two weren't right, maybe a third would be,
even though the conditions were pretty much the same
throughout that entire corner of the continent. I was dredg-
ing a big, dark stone-fly nymph because that's what was supposed to work here, if something was going to work, and I
hooked a good fish. I was standing crotch-deep in the river
and he jumped higher than my head, flashing like chrome in
the sun, and then ran me into the backing. I finally beached
him fifty or sixty yards downstream. He was a good eighteen
inches long, fat and silvery with a slightly kyped jaw. He was
beautiful. He was also foul-hooked under a pectoral fin. Jim
had been fishing upstream, but he trotted down and said,
"Now that's a salmon."

I said, "But he's foul-hooked."

Jim said, "Yeah, that happens."

By then I had gotten myself past the expectation of success
and into the fisherman's eternal riddles: There are fish in here
somewhere, but where? They're in here sometimes, but when?
They're eating something, but what? If this were a koan—and
I'm not sure it isn't—it would be: If the salmon cannot be
caught, how will you catch him?

Imagine the first human to conceive of this. He'd have
dipped a hook in the water and plucked out a fish. People
wouldn't have believed him, so he'd have shown them and it
would have seemed like magic. Some days it still does.

Chapter 3

THIS WAS one of those trips that, before it was over, ate up nearly a thousand miles, five tanks of gas, three quarts of oil, God knows how many cups of coffee, and cost me one sixty-six-dollar speeding ticket from a polite but humorless cop outside Moneta, Wyoming, one of those towns where the elevation exceeds the population by hundreds of times. In this case, 5,428 feet, ten residents. As near as I could tell, there hadn't been a hiding place in the last fifty miles big enough for a jackrabbit, let alone a police car. I wasn't pleased about the ticket, but the cop had apparently come out of thin air and I had to hand it to him.

It's easy to drive too fast across these flat, empty basins between mountain ranges where a trip of any distance can dissolve into a kind of pointless, caffeine-induced speed. It's daylight. You can see for miles. The roads are straight and there doesn't seem to be anything to run into, although the small white crosses along the side of the road suggest otherwise.

Once you slow down closer to the speed limit, you notice more of them.

I was on my way to float the Wind River on the Shoshone and Arapaho reservation with Tom McGuane, Mike Lawson, Jack Dennis, and guide Darren Calhoun. Tom is the novelist whose work I've admired all my adult life and whose fishing books are among the rare few that read like they're true. Mike is the author of the landmark book *Spring Creeks,* but I first knew him as the slow-talking guru of the Henry's Fork of the Snake River in Last Chance, Idaho, and Jack wrote the fly-tying book that was propped open on my desk when I tried to tie my first trout fly sometime in the early 1970s. I've always been impressed by writers and, oddly enough, being a writer myself hasn't tarnished that one bit.

These are men I don't get to see often, but who I know and like, so there were none of the usual worries about celebrity fishing. It's hard to describe and impossible to predict, but there's often some sort of nonsense from the well known. I once fished with a famous angler who was actually a pretty good fisherman, but who only enjoyed catching trout when there was someone nearby who *wasn't* catching them. As for writers, I once met one who claimed that he couldn't start writing a book until he had "dreamed extensively in the voices of all the characters." That kind of thing.

For my own part, I've never been able to manage anything like dignity while fishing and I've never met anyone else who could manage it either. The few who I've seen try all ended up looking like pompous fools, although to their credit, many of them came to realize that and eventually would only fish with *other* pompous fools.

Anyway, I'd never fished the Wind—which is reason enough to go—but Jack had also told me there were some big trout in it. I probably asked "How big?" because that's the automatic response, but I didn't pay attention to the answer because it wouldn't have mattered. As always, we'd go to the river with no clear plan except to fish, and something would either shake out or not.

I stopped in the town of Shoshone and bought my reservation fishing permit at a twenty-four-hour gas station called the Fast Lane. Then I drove the thirty-some miles down the canyon to the motel where we'd check in and meet Darren for a half day shakedown float. I was ahead of schedule, so I drove slowly to calm the road jitters a little and pulled over here and there to look at the water. Stopping to check out the river before you start fishing amounts to a kind of foreplay, but it can also be the longest and best look you'll get. Later on, you can be too busy to take in the view in anything more than quick glances.

The canyon was loose-looking, beige-colored sandstone with its lip weathered into crags and towers, some of which looked like they could topple in a strong breeze. It was cut deeply enough that even in early afternoon most of it was still in shadow. The surrounding landscape was mostly thin grasses, shrubs and rubble rock. There were some scattered pines and junipers, but the trees even a little way up from the river looked dry and desperate and a few were just plain dead, with their needles the color of abandoned iron.

There were stretches where the canyon widened and leveled a bit, but what sticks in my mind are the long narrows where a good-sized river is squeezed into white water and foamy pools that you could never reach on foot. In most places it would be a long, steep scramble from the road to the water, then a grunt up, over and down to the next pool. It would be grueling and there'd be a lot of water you couldn't reach, including some of the best. People do wade-fish this, but apparently not many. In over thirty miles, on a beautiful summer day with the water looking near perfect, I only saw two fishermen, and one was standing by the side of the road scratching his head.

At the motel, we caught up quickly as fishermen can do, even those who haven't seen each other in a long time. How have you been? You're looking good. How was your drive? What do you think, a seven-weight rod and streamers? And Tom had to ask about my elderly pickup, knowing I'm one of those who proudly drive rattletraps to make some obscure populist statement and also to save the cost of a new one to spend instead on guides and fishing tackle. I recited the stats. Fifteen years old, 200,000-some miles, only three minor accidents, decent compression, nobody's gonna steal it and I just got a speeding ticket for doing eighty in a sixty-five zone: proof that my old horse can still run.

Darren turned out to be one of those strapping young guys who is hardworking and earnest, but still has the fully functioning sense of humor that's a must when you deal with fishermen. He runs the guide service in the summer, floating fishermen for trout and white-water types for thrills and chills. He has the only outfit licensed to guide commercially on the reservation, and only reservation residents can float the river on their own, so he has what you'd have to call a lock on some very good water. Lots of things conspire to make the trout in one river bigger than in another, but difficult foot access and very light boat traffic would be two big ones.

In the off-season when he's not guiding, Darren is studying for a degree in psychiatry—looking to "do something with his life" as my father would have said—but the summer job would be good training. Guides get used to seeing raw emotions and exposed insecurities. And really, the only thing a psychiatrist can do that a good guide can't is write prescriptions.

I was a little sorry to hear about this impending career change, for entirely selfish reasons. Most guides—including most of the best—sooner or later move on to something in or out of the fishing business that actually lets them make a living. That's a good thing for them, but they're sorely missed on the river. Then again, if I ever decide I need a shrink, maybe I can find one who started out as a fishing guide.

I don't know enough about white water to guess at the classification numbers of the rapids in the canyon, but some are definitely in the oh-my-god category. You're drifting along casting your streamer to the pockets when you hear the dull roar. When you look downstream, the river just drops from sight and dissolves into spray. Darren slips the raft into a backwater, tells you to put on your life vest and you buckle it all the way to your chin without arguing.

Later in the trip you'll have more confidence and you might even try (usually without success) to play a big trout through the rapids. But as it is, you've only known the man at the oars for an hour. He's done fine in the slower water and he does run a river-rafting outfit, but you still wonder. If you're in the bow of the raft going over that first drop—feet braced on the tube, free hand death-gripping the seat, your back to the guide and the other fisherman in the stern seat—you can come to feel very much alone.

But then everything goes perfectly and you're casting again before you can even appreciate the relief because the good pockets come and go so quickly and you could hook a hog in any one of them. There aren't a whole lot of fish in there, but many of them are big browns and rainbows twenty inches or better, and as often as not you'll only get one good cast per spot.

We fished streamers on that first short float and stayed with them for the next few days, with only a few detours into dry flies in the rare stretches of quiet water. I ended up fishing heavy, lead-eyed Muddlers and sculpins off a short leader on a floating weight-forward line. A longer sink-tip with an un-weighted streamer would have been more graceful, but the idea was to hammer the cast and sink the fly quickly in the small pockets. There was usually no time or room for the long, tantalizing swing. I didn't pay close attention, but I think Jack, Mike, and Tom used similar rigs.

Blow-by-blow accounts of fishing are usually boring to everyone except the fisherman telling the tale, so I'll just say we caught some trout and they were big. Little ones went around fifteen or sixteen inches; bigger ones were twenty-plus and upwards of four pounds. And of course we missed some, although I can't say how many. Sometimes there'd just be a little tick that could have been a half-baked strike from a big trout or the streamer bumping a rock. Other times there was spray and loud splashing and no doubt about it.

We were a little late getting out that first day because of the inevitable confusion generated by two rafts, two guides (Darren and Mike), several cars and a gang of fishermen trying to get organized while carrying on a six-way conversation. So we floated till past dark, derigged by flashlight and ended up getting supper wrapped in cellophane at the all-night gas station across from the motel. There was one evening when we drove to the one actual restaurant in the area and had a good sit-down meal, but the rest of the time we ate microwaved junk and lived with it. There's a basic rule of dining that says, Never eat at a place with gas pumps outside, but it's one of the many rules fishermen regularly break out of necessity.

The next day, back in the canyon, I got my big trout. It was a pretty brown that took the streamer hard and fought it out in a stretch where I didn't have to try and keep him on through a set of class-four rapids. (It was only the second day, but we'd already lost some big trout trying to do just that.) The entire crew of the raft guessed its weight at around seven or eight pounds, so it was probably at least close to that. I mention it only to brag, although I didn't do anything special. He was just the fish that happened to bite on that cast.

We did a couple of days in the canyon, switching around between two rafts and guides so everyone got to fish with everyone else. It was big enough water that we could leapfrog and all meet up from time to time. Breaks and especially lunches tended to go long because the stories were so good and because, coincidentally, the fishing would be pretty slow in midday.

Mike's stories tended to be brief, plainspoken, light on ridicule and to the point. Jack's were long, incredibly detailed and filled with asides that sometimes all came together at the end and sometimes didn't. Tom's were spare, angular and character-based, like his books. McGuane has the most extensive vocabulary of anyone I know, but he doesn't use it as a weapon. Sometimes you can see him struggling to tone it down a little when he's talking to ordinary people who don't have dictionaries handy.

All the stories were either about fishing or at least had some fishing in them, but some of those Tom and I told also contained some counterculture shenanigans that now and then left the rest of the group gazing at us wide-eyed. If nothing else, it might have been more training for Darren's future practice: proof that people could act foolishly for a very long time, end up only mildly impaired and not regret any of it.

Naturally, all of us had those spates where we got strikes but couldn't hook up. My turn came on the last day. We'd checked out of the motel and driven far upstream, above the canyon, where we split up to fish two different stretches of the upper river. I was with Lawson and one of Darren's young guides who was also named Mike, so when I said, "Hey, Mike," they'd both answer.

The canyon we'd been fishing for the last few days was below a dam, so the flow was controlled. It hadn't seemed low, but then I'd never seen it before so I didn't know how it was supposed to look, and when a river gets squeezed through a narrow gorge, a comparatively small amount of water can still seem like a lot.

The river upstream was a whole other story. It flowed down an open, gently sloping valley with long views of grass and shrubland scattered with cottonwoods, sort of a North American version of the Serengeti. The river ran in long, lazy bends with sloping cobbled banks on the inside and deep undercuts outside. The river looked fine, but shrunken between its wide banks. Mike the guide said it was lower than usual, and that we'd have to get out and drag the raft over some shallow spots, but that it was still fishing well. It was the same story I'd been hearing all over the West throughout the drought: It's okay now, but if it gets much lower we could start to have a problem.

I landed some trout early on, including a beautiful five-pound rainbow that jumped once straight up, then tore off in a series of porpoising arcs. Then I proceeded to miss strike after strike over the next few hours while Lawson caught quite a few trout. He offered some helpful suggestions, but of course there was nothing anyone could do.

I went through the usual agonies. Am I setting too soon or too late? Too softly or too hard? Could I get more solid takes if I stripped the fly slower—or maybe faster? I *am* getting the strikes, so I'm almost there. It's just some little thing . . . Later in the day I began to hook a few fish again without doing anything differently. If I live to be a hundred, I'll never understand how that happens.

In the first bend pool after our lunch break, Lawson hooked a fourteen- or fifteen-inch rainbow on a streamer, and when he got it close to the boat a big brown trout flashed it, and then flashed it again. I won't guess at how big this thing was, but it was big. Way bigger than anything we'd seen there. Big enough that it took an extra second for it to register that this was actually a fish and not something like a curious beaver.

The guide and I were standing there with our mouths open when Lawson said, "Cast to him." So I did. On the second cast the brown wheeled and went for my streamer. I don't know if he actually ate it or just bumped it, but of course I missed him, and then he was gone. For the next half hour we told stories about one fish eating another off a fisherman's line in both fresh and salt water, beginning slowly with bass eating bluegills and ending with hundred-pound tarpon being bitten in half by giant sharks.

At the end of that last day, we split up at the Crowheart Store to go our separate ways, Tom to Montana, Mike and Jack to Idaho and Wyoming respectively, me south at least in the direction of Colorado. In the store I poured a cup of sour, lukewarm coffee and when I went to pay for it the guy said, "Aw, that's okay. I was gonna throw it out anyway." I drank half of it and threw the rest out myself.

The Crowheart Store is in sight of Crowheart Butte—a local landmark—and a few days earlier I'd asked about the name. According to the story, back in the old days the Shoshone and Crow chiefs decided to have it out once and for all on top of this flat-topped hill. The Shoshone chief not only won the fight, he cut out the Crow chief's heart and ate it, making a lasting impression.

When I got out on the paved highway, I began feeling for the ideal speed that was fast enough for the wobble in the truck's front end to level out, but not so fast that the leaky sunroof would begin to howl in the wind. This invariably works out to be either ten miles an hour under the speed limit or ten miles over.

It was late and I was tired, so that night I only planned to go as far as the first motel. In the morning I'd decide whether to go on home or maybe stop and fish some of the several dozen trout streams I'd cross depending on the route I picked. On the way up, a few streams had looked a little too low to fish well, but the rest had seemed okay, given the quick look you get as you drive over the bridge. But at the moment I didn't know where I'd go or when I'd get there: a feeling that makes me happier than almost anything else.

And then somewhere around Bull Lake Creek, I remembered something Tom had said one morning after one of us had just finished yet another long story about the old days: "We have a hundred and fifty years of fishing between us," he said, "but only a short time to figure out why." It was a good line; good enough to momentarily stop three chronic talkers in their tracks.

Chapter 4

PLAYING SOME of those big trout on the Wind River is among the dozens of images that will pop to the surface the next time someone asks me why I fish. Especially in the steep canyon water, there were times when the boat was inexorably going one way, while a fish weighing several pounds was either going the other way or stubbornly staying where he was. There could be a feeling of hopelessness that was often justified, and although there were times when there was a right thing to do and you were able to do it, getting one to the net always seemed to involve at least a little bit of luck.

That's where the whole aesthetic of the big ones comes from: With smaller fish, the hookup can seem to come very near the end of the story, but with a big fish, setting the hook is just the opening scene.

The fly-fishing instructors I know tell me that the single hardest thing in the sport to teach is how to play a fish. That's because you can practice tying knots while sitting in an easy chair and you can practice casting on a lawn, but to practice playing a fish you basically have to have a fish on, and then it's not practice, it's for real.

A dog, it turns out, is a poor substitute for a fish. One winter, at the Blue Quill Fly Shop in Evergreen, Colorado, a few of us went out back and tried playing Dixie on an eight-weight fly rod. Dixie is a lean, young, fun-loving forty-pound mutt who had done this before. It's a game with the humans where she's the center of attention, so she either enjoys it or at least doesn't mind. (If the dog *did* mind, you'd not only never do it again, you'd also feed her treats and rub her tummy for days trying to win back her affection.)

Anyway, Dixie's owner tied the leader to the dog's collar, handed the rod to my friend A. K. Best and then threw an old slobbered-on tennis ball far out into an open field. A.K. said it felt just like the first run of a big striped bass.

Naturally, I had to try it, and when the dog took off I instinctively dipped the rod tip and even felt a little of that helplessness that grips you when the reel starts to scream and you think you've hooked something you might not be able to land. But then Dixie just picked up the ball and trotted back faster than I could reel in line, so it was sort of anticlimactic. Finally someone wandered out and said, "You guys haven't been fishing for a while, have you?" I suddenly felt embarrassed and went inside for some coffee.

Playing fish is something most of us had to learn the hard way. I vaguely remember that my first few fish on a fly rod came in pretty clumsily when they came in at all, and I even had the benefit of some prior experience. Before I took up fly fishing, I had graduated from hoisting bluegills from farm ponds with a cane pole to playing bass and pike on a solid fiberglass bait-casting rod and level-wind reel, so I at least understood the principle of the thing.

Still, all my struggles up till then had been toward hooking a fish with a fly rod, but I hadn't given much thought to what would happen next. So there I was with the rod in one hand and all that loose line in the other, wondering why a two-handed species would invent an instrument that takes three hands to operate. I don't remember what I did before I learned to snub the line under the index finger of my rod hand, but I've heard some great stories from guides about what others have done.

There was the guy who shoved the loose line in his pants pocket, the guy who held it in his teeth, one who stood on it and several who just went hand over hand down the rod and on out the line to the fish. I'm sure they've all gotten better at it by now and have forgotten their early flops as conveniently as I've forgotten mine, although of course the stories will live on forever in the places where guides gather.

There's some controversy over whether it's best to play a fish by stripping line with your line hand or by getting it on the reel, but I find that the fish usually makes that decision for me. If he pulls out all my loose line, then he's on the reel and that's how I play him. If not, I just strip him in.

Then again, sometimes I'll have a lot of loose line at my feet when I hook a big fish close in that just starts splashing and wallowing. If I think I have time (and how would I know that?) I might try to quickly get my line back on the reel because, although the fish isn't doing much at the moment, he probably will be as soon as he grasps the problem and gets his bearings.

Reeling up the slack can be especially tempting if I'm

standing up to my armpits in a bush or on a beaver dam that's bristling with sharp sticks that will surely grab the loose line. I've had it work, but I've also had it go horribly wrong because if a fish is ever going to do something sudden and unexpected, it'll be when you're not ready.

I *will* say that stripping in loose coils of line instead of reeling vastly increases your chances of snagging that line on sticks, twigs, branches, rocks, burrs, thorns, forceps, hip-boot straps, suspender buckles, watchbands, gravel guards, zipper pulls, vest-pocket flaps, shirt buttons, belt loops, wading staffs, oars, canoe paddles, cameras, landing nets, wading shoes and/or anchor ropes. I speak from experience.

I still reel with my casting hand because when I took up the sport, virtually all American and English reels came right-handed and that's just the way it was done. It means I have to switch hands when a fish goes on the reel, but I've been doing that for so long now I don't even notice when it happens. They say you can lose fish when you switch hands, but I don't think that's ever happened to me, although I've lost fish in every other possible way.

I've also been told that I'm old-fashioned because I switch over and reel with my rod hand, but I usually let that slide. If anyone wants to believe that's the most old-fashioned thing about me, fine.

You could say that playing little fish is easier than playing big ones and not be far wrong, but you can never be too sure about that. I've lost hot little foot-long brookies in fast, brushy creeks and I've also landed great big rainbows—supposedly good fighters—that wore themselves out by swimming in splashy, dim-witted circles right under the rod tip. Every hookup is different, and one of the most delicious moments in fishing is when the line goes tight and you wait to see what the fish wants to do so you can either let him do it or try to stop him, depending on which seems best.

Unless there's a good reason not to, I'll let a fish run if it wants to so it'll wear itself out quicker and because it's just such a pretty sight. I also insist on using a reel that clicks—the louder the better—because a fish that runs without the accompaniment of a screaming reel won't cause anyone to look in the direction of the noise and think, That guy has a nice fish on. I'll drop the rod tip so the rod bends more toward the handle than the tip—"playing it off the butt," as they say—and then at the end of the run I'll usually flop the rod over parallel to the water to turn the fish in whichever direction I want him to go.

Sometimes it's possible to stop a fish dead in his tracks going straight away, but it's almost always better to turn him because it keeps the fight going and because you're less likely to break a tippet or bend open a hook. A fish can only go the way he's facing, so all you have to do is nudge his head around a little bit to start him turning, and there's a lot of steering room. If you have a nine-foot rod and your arms are a little over two feet from shoulder to fist, you have an arc of at least twenty-two feet to play with if you stand in one place, a little more if you lean and a lot more if you move.

In a lake it might not matter which way a fish turns unless he's heading for a snag, but in a river I'll usually try to turn him upstream so he's fighting the current as well as me. That's textbook advice and I always try it, but most times it doesn't work. Hooked fish want to go downstream, either because it's easier or because they instinctively understand that the weight of moving water gives them an advantage.

If a heavy fish gets downstream—and he will if he wants

to—it's best if you can go down there and get below him so he'll be fighting back against the current again, but be careful of running down the bank after a fish. I *have* caught a few that would have been worth a broken leg, but the catch is, if you break your leg you won't land the fish.

When a fish is going one way, I try to put pressure on him in the opposite direction to make him work harder, and when he turns, I turn. That keeps him working against the pull of the line (pulling on a fish in the direction he's already going just lets him rest). I think it also keeps him confused. Whichever way he goes, the pull is always from behind. Pretty soon he runs out of things to try. The more often you can turn a fish, the quicker you can get his head up and land him.

Landing fish quickly means they won't be as tired, so they're more likely to survive when you release them. It also gives the fish less time to throw the hook, break the tippet or wrap you around a snag. The fishermen I know who land the most fish are the ones who play them the hardest.

That's why I seldom fish with a rod lighter than a five-weight and don't care for the ultralight rods in one, two, and three-weight. A rod that's too light won't handle wind, can't cast long distances, won't handle large flies and, most importantly, can't play a big fish with enough authority.

That last moment when the fish is right at the net is the most crucial. It's almost over, you're a little impatient and there's a temptation to pull a little too hard or reach a little too far with the landing net. If the fish bolts or shakes his head at the last second the hook can be thrown or the tippet can be broken. You hear a lot of stories about the big fish that was lost right at the guy's feet. It's pretty common.

When a fish is within inches of your net, you can clearly

see how big he is and your mind races ahead to when he's already caught, so when something gnarly happens you have to rewind back to the present. That can take just long enough for the fish to be gone. Of course it's best to stay cool and collected when things begin to happen quickly. On the other hand, if you don't get excited, why even bother fishing?

It's great when a fish jumps. It's just plain pretty and with some real big ones it could be the only look you get before you reel in your limp line. You might brag about how many times a fish jumped, especially if you land it. A lot of big fish are lost when they jump and there's the old saw about "bowing" to the fish when it comes out of the water. You lower the rod tip so that if the fish lands on your leader when it splashes back into the water, the slack will be off and he'll be less likely to break it. It's called bowing because it looks like a kind of salute.

This apparently started with Atlantic salmon and barbed hooks, sometimes doubles or even trebles. It's probably less of a sure thing with barbless hooks where a tight line is more important, but it still works, especially on big fish and not-so-heavy tippets.

I always try to avoid stalemates, like when a fish gets below you in a current and hangs there, or swims to a deep hole to sulk. The best strategy is to work your way downstream—always keeping the line tight—and then apply more pressure, hoping he'll take off up the current.

I've heard of other solutions. A man once told me you can get a fish running back upstream by throwing out loops of line that belly out down current and then tighten. When the fish feels the tug from below, he runs back upstream. It sounds like something that would work better in theory than in practice. I've never tried it.

Holding a tight line and thumping on the butt of the rod with your free hand can work—the vibration annoys the fish, they say—but it's not guaranteed. I've heard of Atlantic-salmon fishermen throwing rocks at sulking fish to get them moving again. I tried that once with a big trout. I don't recommend it.

It may not always be clear what to do, but I know I have to do *something*. As someone once said, "Either land 'em or lose 'em, but don't screw around with 'em."

But then not screwing around with 'em is easier in some situations than in others. Catching big fish on extremely light tackle takes a lot of skill and is sometimes unavoidable, as when five-pound trout are sipping size-22 mayflies, but when large trout are in the mix I try to use the stoutest rod and the heaviest tippet I can get away with. Of course it's possible to land large, heavy trout on something like a two-weight rod and 7x tippet, but by the time most of us have managed that, we've played the fish nearly to death and it may well die after it's released. The way I see it, ultralight tackle makes real sense only for small fish or big ones you plan to kill and eat.

It's all basic strategy; all easy to forget in the heat of the moment when the thing you've tried so long and hard to get looks like it's getting away. Even if you've never fished before, that's bound to be a familiar feeling.

For me, the toughest part of playing fish is that tendency to panic. The bigger the fish the worse it gets, but in the right mood I can come unglued over an eight-inch trout. It happens a few times every season. For unknown reasons, I forget everything and just lock up, and in the space of a few seconds I make the entire journey from "Oh boy I got one!" to "I am a worthless piece of crap."

I blame that on the adventure fishing stories I read as a kid in the 1950s in which playing a fish was always portrayed as hand-to-hand combat to the death: exactly the kind of thing you want to hear when you're twelve years old. Now I know—at least in my better moments—that it's more cagey and underhanded and that someone who's very good at playing fish on a fly rod would also probably be a good con man, pickpocket or politician. You don't make a new reality: You just nudge the one that's already there in a slightly different direction and then let things play out. If you have to think of playing fish in military terms, consider the advice Sun Tzu gives in *The Art of War*, written in 500 B.C.: "An army turns from strength and attacks emptiness." Sun Tzu is said to have won great battles without ever fighting the enemy. They wore themselves out trying to attack him, but he was never there.

Once you've played a few fish well, especially some big, strong ones in tough spots, it begins to look a little more like applied common sense—let him run when you have to and pull him back when you can—but it's still something you have to learn out on the water with live fish and real current, snags, rocks and weeds. It's rare to do anything right the first couple of times, and most of us end up losing the first few really big fish we hook, as well as a fair number of subsequent ones. Eventually we get over it.

I once had a beginning fly fisher out in my canoe on a lake that was known for its trophy-sized rainbows. She wasn't a rank beginner—she'd fished for a few seasons and had landed plenty of small stream trout—but this was her first shot at a real pig. After trolling around for a while with a size-14 damsel nymph, she hooked a heavy fish and started reeling it in, but when it made a good strong run she kept right on reeling and broke it off.

I tied a fresh fly on her leader and went through the drill: Reel him in when you can, but when he pulls back too hard, let him run. "How hard is too hard?" she asked, which of course is the central question. All I could come up with was, "You figure that out eventually," which was true, but not immediately helpful.

She took my advice and let the next fish run. It ran halfway across the lake on a slack line and threw the hook while I was trying to decide what to say and how to say it calmly.

That's why I'm such a poor guide: I either yell and sputter or just sit there tongue-tied while everything goes to hell. Luckily, I almost never guide, and on the rare occasions when I do, it's always for free so people can't demand their money back.

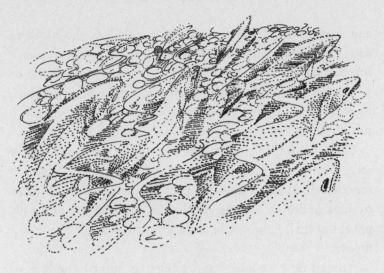

Chapter 5

THEY SAY people travel in order to experience the enormity of the world, but there's also something to be said for being mindful of the enormity of your own home region. In my case, that's a few hundred square miles of the northern Colorado Rockies that I think I know intimately, but still couldn't properly explore in a dozen lifetimes.

That's why I do almost all my midseason fishing in the local high country within day-trip range of home, trying out a few new spots every year, visiting the old favorites to see how they're doing, and just generally wallowing in thirty-some years' worth of accumulated familiarity. Fishing three or four days a week on average through the summer, I find this a pleasant chore that usually takes no less than two months, but during the drought it stretched out closer to three, with most of the extra time coming on the early end.

My house sits at right around 6,000 feet above sea level,

and at roughly 7,000 feet you begin to get above the last dams and headgates to where the water stays in the streams where it belongs. Depending on which drainage you choose, it can be a one-way drive of anywhere from fifteen minutes to three hours to reach a place where all that's asked of water is that it run downhill and keep the trout wet.

Gary Snyder once said that historically, mountains were seen as a refuge for outlaws and mystics, but he forgot to mention that they can also be partially droughtproof. I refuse to think of fishing as escapism, but the idea that you can easily get above it all—physically and otherwise—is still sort of addictive.

Around here, at least—and I think in most mountainous regions—the term "high country" means steep little streams filled with small trout, and that's the expectation you bring to this kind of fishing. An old friend (now deceased) used to say, "The archetypal trout is ten inches long at maturity. That's your benchmark." Aside from being a little pretentious, that always sounded about right to me. These small, high-altitude trout streams are among the wildest water we have left in the West and they're also what we have the most of. There are hundreds of miles of them just in my home county—most of them public, many of them roadless in their higher reaches. They're filled with trout of various species that, overall, probably average out to around ten inches or a little less. You'll sometimes hear waters like this described as marginal or second-class, but you develop a taste for the fishing the way you do for one of those regional cuisines that arise in a place where there isn't much to eat.

But naturally there are exceptions to small fish size, and fishermen do live for exceptions. Over the years I've been to a few rare places in the regional mountains where a pool, or a series of pools, or even a quarter mile of stream holds some unusually large trout. They'll be maybe fifteen inches long and there won't be just the lone big fish—which can happen any-where—but several of them: maybe one or two to every pool for an eighth of a mile or more.

I'm not sure what's going on here. All these places were re-mote, but that can't be the whole story because there are vast stretches of equally remote water where the fish size is just what you'd expect. It's just a mystery—the kind that makes you want to fish every inch of every stream you can find.

And the headwater lakes will also sometimes grow big fish. I remember a small one at around 10,000 feet in a Colorado wilderness area that had a handful of enormous cutthroat trout. They'd been planted as fingerlings by the Division of Wildlife in hopes that they'd establish themselves as a self-sus-taining population, but there was almost no spawning habitat, so the fish lived their lives—happily, you assume—but gradu-ally died out without ever reproducing.

By the time I got there, six or seven years after the stock-ing, there were only a few trout left, but they'd grown to great size. That's what I'd hoped. It was also the gist of the rumor I'd heard and the stocking records made it sound plausible. The few trout I spotted in the clear water looked like they'd have easily gone twenty-four inches, but the one thing I hadn't foreseen was that I wouldn't be able to catch them. They cruised along slowly in about three feet of clear water and they wouldn't look at any fly I threw at them.

I'm sure I was discouraged at the time—it was a killer hike for no fish—but now I remember it as the kind of fleetingly beautiful sight I might like to remember on my deathbed: giant trout cruising by in the clear water like pictures at an exhibition, and just that untouchable. I naturally think that now that I'm older and wiser I could catch some of them, but of course I'll never know. Unless they've restocked the lake by airdrop, those fish are now long gone.

So it does happen—the big fish do turn up now and then—but usually as you head uphill away from the rivers and into the headwaters, the streams shrink, so do the trout, and that seems okay.

I learned to fly-fish on small mountain creeks in Colorado and I got used to nine- and ten-inch trout early on. My first few fish on a fly rod came hard, and when they finally did start to come, ten-inch trout were just fine. My favorites were brook trout and cutthroats, but there was nothing wrong with the browns and rainbows either, and I soon learned that my actual favorite fish was whatever I happened to be catching at the moment. Whatever the fish turned out to be, they were pretty, scrappy and perfectly in scale with the small waters where they lived. I found that I'd happily walk five miles uphill to catch ten-inch trout, and if I thought they'd be twelve or thirteen inches, I'd hike eight miles in the rain.

I couldn't get enough of it. Once I quit a job specifically because working cut too deeply into the fishing time. I had this adolescent idea that an entire life could be used up by fishing, good books and a few other pleasant things like sex and bird-watching. I now know that was naively idealistic, but I still haven't given up on it. Anyway, that was in the late 1960s and early '70s when all kinds of dangerously strange and subversive things were happening and if you felt moved to push against the apparent boundaries, you'd find that many of them weren't boundaries at all. My family worried that I'd rot my brain and ruin my life, but they never suspected that trout fishing would be the cause.

• • •

I'm constantly trying out new streams in the region because it's just always good to fish any new water. There's a strong sense of exploration and discovery even if fishermen by the thousands have been there before. But I do get a very specific buzz when I try a secluded mountain creek for the first time.

I was trying to place the feeling. It's hard to explain—as feelings usually are—but it seemed detached from actual time, like a family story you've heard so often you think you remember the event, even though the chronology tells you it had to have happened before you were born.

It turned out to be the rush I used to get when I was young and carefree and either quit or was fired from a job I needed, but didn't like. The sudden freedom would produce a kind of simple euphoria: Good, bad or indifferent, something new was about to happen. That feeling preceded some of the best and worst times of my life and for a while I became hooked on the notion of doing something, even if it was wrong, just to shake things up.

Shaking things up concluded in all sorts of ways, but it usually started with days of fishing, even if that's not why I quit or lost the job in the first place. This would usually be in small mountain streams near home where I would happily trust in my blue-collar luck. I knew I wouldn't win the lottery or find a rich, older woman to be my patron, but I also knew I could find work before the money ran out.

I finally located the feeling when a friend told me he was going to quit his job. There were some logical reasons—the kind not even your parents could argue with—but there was also the suggestion that just being alive had gotten to be an itch he couldn't quite scratch from his current position. He said the plan was to go steelhead fishing for six weeks to clear his head before he worried too much about what came next, and I envied him for that. I sometimes think my life has gotten a little too orderly, but then not long ago a friend said my career showed about the same level of planning as a boulder rolling downhill and I felt better because a boulder rolling downhill ends up exactly where it's supposed to be.

My friend with the job hadn't exactly asked my advice (he'd already made the decision) but he did ask me what I thought. I had to quit job after job before my own head finally started to clear, but when it did I had become a guy who makes an uncertain, but pleasant living writing about fishing: the kind of thing you can stumble into when you're at loose ends. I told him I thought it was a good plan—especially the part about the six weeks of steelheading.

But that kind of nostalgia aside, I don't think I fish these small streams to do anything as tawdry as reclaim my lost youth. Youth is still in there somewhere, informing the older man when he needs to be reminded of something, but otherwise bowing to greater experience. I've also learned that life is equally uncertain whether you quit the job or keep it; there are just ways in which that can be either more or less fun.

The small streams in my local high country tend to be mostly "pocket water," one of those terms fly fishers toss around pretty loosely. It really just means current broken by obstacles, but in the Rocky Mountains you picture loud creeks that run in long, complicated riffles and then steepen into stair-step plunge pools sometimes just a few degrees short of waterfalls.

When I began fishing in the mountains, this stuff was so different from the placid water where I caught bass and bluegills as a kid in the Midwest that I ignored it at first. I actually walked past miles of what I now recognize as beautiful pocket water looking for the few deep, smooth pools that I thought were proper places for trout to live.

Naturally, the rough canyon stretches I once thought would be poor trout habitat turned out to be some of the best. The boulders, deadfalls, logjams, plunge pools and fast currents all amount to the kind of cover trout like; the falling water stays cool and well oxygenated; and the jumbled stream beds have lots of surface area for aquatic bugs to live in. The really ragged stretches, with a few small, foamy slicks scattered around in otherwise white water, is now what I like best.

I learned to fish pocket water through a process of mimicry: by watching people who were better at it than I was and trying to do what they did. They were fishing the roughest water, crawling around on boulders and reaching over fallen logs to make short, choppy casts. They were fishing close in, sometimes with just the leader and a few feet of line out. Their drifts were accurate but short: six inches and a few seconds at best. They were catching the hell out of trout.

These weren't the long, sinuous casts I saw pictured in the fishing magazines, and they weren't the huge trout I saw in the grip-and-grin hero shots either. I began to think the magazine stuff was a separate sport practiced by older, richer guys, and in a way I was right.

Anyway, I tried it and it worked—not great at first, but better and better the more I kept at it. But then that's just how you learn to fish: by piecing together what trout are all about through the accumulation of detail, one trout at a time, season after season. As Annie Dillard once said of the process of observation, "If you can't see the forest for the trees, then look at the trees. When you've looked at enough trees, you've seen a forest."

For years I fished pretty quickly up these mountain creeks,

making a few casts to every likely-looking spot and then moving on, calling my shots and covering water. I'd gotten it into my head that if you didn't get a strike with five good drifts to one spot, you wouldn't get one at all. (The growing season is short in the high country and the fish are hungry and eager.) I thought of this as efficiency rather than impatience or, worse yet, the all-too-common lust for a large body count. I released all my fish except for an occasional brace of brook trout for supper, but there was still a competitive edge. Catch-and-release fishing could have changed the sport into something less macho and more philosophical, but in many cases all it's done is allow us to brag about bigger numbers.

But then sometimes I'd make a few extra casts to water I thought was pretty marginal, just to see what would happen, and get a strike I didn't expect. That happened often enough that I finally began to slow down, not only fishing more water, but also making more casts. I started getting strikes on the tenth or the fifteenth drift instead of the fourth or fifth. Who knows why? Maybe the trout took that long to make up their minds, or maybe they were looking the other way when the fly went over the first fourteen times. Even when you catch the fish, there's still a lot you don't know.

Not all of those trout were slightly bigger than the rest, but a few were, so maybe that was it: another year in the water, an extra inch or two in length, a little bit more caution. Most of these streams still don't see a lot of fishing pressure, but like trout streams everywhere, they see more than they used to, and in some cases what were once my own little secrets are now just what any well-informed local fisherman knows.

On average, I was catching just as many trout in shorter stretches of stream and a few of them were bigger. It occurred to me that, the way things are now, being just as happy with a little less was a damned useful skill.

Last summer, on a small creek near home, I was fishing along at about the same pace that an archeologist sifts dirt, taking all the time in the world so as not to miss anything. I cast a dry fly to an eddy about two feet across with a slowly revolving current and found that by following the fly with the rod tip, I could get an endless, elliptical drag-free float. I was so delighted that I left the fly on the water for a long time. Maybe ten minutes, maybe more. I should have timed it. All I know is, my arm finally got tired and began to shake, so when a brown trout calmly ate the fly, it was only reflex that let me set the hook.

He turned out to be sixteen inches long, the biggest trout I've ever seen come out of that creek. In the scale of a stream no more than two rod lengths wide, he might as well have been a salmon, and he must have watched that size-14 Hare's Ear Parachute circle his pool forty times.

That had been one of those blissfully slow-paced days where I wouldn't so much as take a step until I'd made many casts to every spot I could reach. In a long afternoon, I covered a stretch of stream you'd measure in hundreds of yards instead of fractions of a mile. The big brown trout had been the fish that made the day, but I'd caught many more—so many I quit early, broke down my rod and strolled slowly back to the truck looking for bolete mushrooms. There weren't many because of the dry summer, but I found three perfect ones with nut-brown heads the size of doorknobs.

In my brightest moments, I think slowing down like that has opened huge new vistas on my old home water. It's like a friendship that not only lasts, but gets better against the odds. Or maybe it's like writing, where there's always either something new to say or at least new ways to say the same old things.

Then again, I have to wonder if maybe it's age that's slowed me down a little, although that's not as obvious as I once thought it would be. I started fishing these creeks in my twenties. Now I'm thirty years past that with an acquired taste for ibuprofen, convinced that, for this kind of fishing, at least, slow and methodical beats relentless. Years of being relentless do exact a price, but that's just something some men do. We pick out lives that we know will beat us up, and then, somewhere in our late fifties, we begin to wonder how the hell we got so beat-up.

I suppose fishing in steep country does become a kind of litmus test for aging. One winter I got pretty sick. (Don't worry, I won't go into too much detail. If there's one rule of conversation it's that no one really wants to hear about your operation.) Briefly, my gall bladder went haywire and turned into a raging gut infection. There was a week in the hospital during which I lost twenty pounds I couldn't spare, then an operation and then a recuperation lasting several months that finally led to a complete recovery.

That happened in the winter and all that time I had my eye on the coming fishing season, which would start early because of the low snowpack. I did the prescribed physical therapy and then some, hitting it so hard that I hurt my back and had to do therapy for that, too. I walked daily, adding distance in small but impatient increments. I joined a gym. For a while, with breaks to write and tie flies, putting myself back together became a full-time job. During that time a writer friend described me in print as "frail." At first I felt like hitting him for it, but I knew I was too frail to throw anything but a sissy punch.

Toward the end of my convalescence, Vince, our mutual friend Doug Powell and I hiked into a small but steep stream canyon nearby that was one of those open secrets: a place everyone knows about, but not everyone fishes. I was feeling frisky enough by comparison with the previous months, but I wasn't what you could call back in shape and before we even made it down to the stream I realized I'd bitten off more than I could chew. I'd gotten a little tired walking *down*hill and it was going to be a long, steep, uphill grind to get back out after a day of fishing. I wasn't absolutely sure I could manage it.

I remember that we did a lot of rock scrambling through some narrow parts of the canyon and that farther up in there we got some very respectable brown trout on Pale Morning Dun dry flies. I also remember coming on a stand of magnificent mature ponderosa pines 150 feet tall with trunks four feet thick; what the old loggers called "yellow barks," even though the bark is actually more of a rusty orange. These old trees used to be fairly common along the Front Range, but most of them died out during the pine-bark-beetle infestation in the 1970s when I and many other young guys at loose ends made a good living cutting them.

It was a nice double dip. We'd get paid to cut the trees through the summer, then the state guys would spray the logs to kill the beetle larvae, and then we'd come back in the fall and sell the firewood. It didn't work as an eradication program—the beetles were only stopped by an explosion in the woodpecker population—but it was good work and good money and in those years I was probably as hard and strong as I've ever been.

Good work and good money is an uncommon mix. I thoroughly enjoyed it then and I sometimes miss it now: not only the hard physical labor, but the long succession of days where my sole purpose was to drop trees and stack logs. (Of course I'm happy to be making a living fishing and writing about it, but it's a life that sometimes lacks simplicity.)

But then once the big old trees were gone I immediately started to miss them. The good work was over and without the old-growth ponderosas, the woods suddenly looked as sterile as those American suburbs where there are no old people. When we found that remnant stand of them alive and well down in that canyon, I got a wet lump in my throat that I had to force back out of embarrassment. And although I'm not exactly a tree hugger, I would have hugged one of those old trees if I thought it would notice. At the time this felt like a deeply complicated emotion, but in the end it just boiled down to feeling sorry for myself. In the months it took me to get sick and then get well again, I suppose it had to happen at least once.

Of course I did make it back out of the canyon, but it was grueling. When the two younger guys noticed me falling behind, they charitably slowed their pace and even stopped and pretended to look at wildflowers once to let me rest. I was a little embarrassed, but I still appreciated the gesture.

But my eventual recovery was complete, as I said. By the middle of that fishing season, I felt like I've always felt, which is about the same way I did when I was twenty. (Okay, if I went to bed at age twenty and woke up at fifty-seven, I'd be able to tell the difference, but time softens incremental changes.) I was no longer mad at my friend for the "frail" comment because he was right, but I did still feel like marching him up a trail at 10,000 feet until he keeled over from altitude sickness. He lives in Maine, near sea level. It wouldn't be that hard.

Oddly enough, the only things that had made me feel old

that season happened later in the normal course of things and had nothing at all to do with hiking, fishing or general health and everything to do with vanity, which in most of us is a kind of emotional bladder that has to be drained periodically anyway.

One time I'd taken a writing break and gone to town for coffee, and I arrived at the door of the coffee shop at the same moment as a very young, very pretty, very pregnant woman. She held the door for me and said, "Go ahead, sir."

And then not long after that a local writer interviewed me for an article he was doing on the politics of water in Colorado, thinking I must be an expert on such things because I wrote books about fly-fishing. In the story, he described me as having "skinny legs, a scraggly gray beard and more lines in his face than a topographic map." I went into the bathroom with my reading glasses, searched the mirror for wrinkles and, by God, there they were. Funny I'd never noticed them before.

Chapter 6

FOR MOST of us, fishing is a more or less social sport. I've met people who would no sooner go fishing by themselves than they would have gone to their senior prom without a date. I've even seen people give it up entirely when an old fishing partner died or moved away.

And I have to say I value my own small handful of fishing friends, if only because they're such a rare breed. That is, they're people who fish well—but not so much better than me that it's humbling—and who have been able to put up with me far longer than the wives, girlfriends and non-angling friends who have fallen away over the same years. In some ways, fishing with a good, familiar partner has many of the best attributes of fishing by yourself. There can be long silences that aren't awkward and you hardly ever have to stop and explain yourself. Sometimes you'll only see the guy three or four times all day—and even then only at a distance—although later you'll say the two of you "went fishing together."

But there's still something about actually getting out alone. I could say I need the time to work things out, but that wouldn't be quite accurate, even though the effect can be the same, as when you hike up a creek with a problem and hike back out with a solution without ever having thought about it.

It was in late July when I went to fish a stretch of a local creek that just came up in conversation one day the way these things do. Mike Price and I were fishing another stream in the same general area and got to wondering how long it had been since we'd been up there. It had to be, what? Ten years? Twelve? No telling, but it had definitely been a while. This sort of thing had been happening more and more often in the last few years as we'd neglected old water to try out new streams and then felt we had to go back to the old stuff again to see how it was holding up. Being a savvy local fisherman can become a full-time job, but then someone has to do it.

Anyway, this one nagged at me until, three days later, I decided I had to fish it right now. I didn't go alone out of any particular longing for solitude, but because Mike happened to be working the day shift that week and no one else was around.

I hiked in on the well-groomed trail where the national park rangers had gone in early in the season to chainsaw the deadfalls so tourists wouldn't trip and sue. There were fresh-cut trunks abutting the trail here and there, and the sharp smell of pine sap was still strong. It was about a mile and a half to the spot where the path loops above and away from the creek, while the stream itself snakes off upstream in the other direction up a rough little canyon.

The casual half-day anglers fish below here (some days I'm

one of them), the more gung ho bust on up to the lakes miles above and the sightseers stick to the trail, which loops conveniently past all the waterfalls. It's the kind of place that diverts the easy traffic and where the trout probably aren't big enough for too many fishermen to make the extra effort. Price and I discovered it independently before we knew each other, but we'd both used the same logic: This could be a place where most people don't go, therefore . . .

The slope there wasn't too steep, but the footing was uncertain and there were lots of boulders and deadfalls to work around. There are parts of this country where you really get a sense that you're in a steep, young range of mountains that has only recently begun to fall apart, and this is one of them. Some of this country looks like recent wreckage, and in geologic terms it is.

I wanted to put in some distance before I started fishing, but I also wanted to go carefully. When I'm out alone, I always arrange for someone to know where I am in case I get into trouble, but that's not foolproof. In this case, no one would worry until hours past dark, and then it would be the next day before I could expect anyone to come looking. It's best to take the usual precautions and then try hard not to require rescue.

But I guess that's one of the lures of fishing alone. In one way, you can be more outside yourself because you can see something beautiful or interesting without immediately having to frame the sentence it would take to point it out to someone else. But then you're more inside yourself, too, because you have to be more careful—looking before you put your foot down to make sure there's something under it, for instance.

Just a few days before, I'd taken a hard fall in a four-inch-deep riffle with a rock bottom: the kind where one second you're upright and going about your business and the next you're wet and in pain and wondering what's broken. I'd spotted a trout rising in a back eddy and I was working out line for the cast while wading upstream for a better angle. I managed to trip over the only rock within sixty feet that was bigger than a golf ball. As it turned out, I wasn't hurt (if you don't count pride) but it must have looked bad because no one laughed until later. Still, it was good to know there were two friends along who could have gone for help if I'd needed it.

I also enjoy where my mind goes when I'm fishing alone, which is usually nowhere in particular and by a predictable route. I start out thinking about specific things, which multiply as I focus on them, but then those things begin to run together in the same way the individual noises that make up the sound of a current dissolve into that one, long whoosh you eventually stop hearing. Either the mind empties or it gets so full it might as well be empty. Something like that. I only think about it afterward. If I thought about it while it was happening, it wouldn't happen.

This was a regulation small trout stream at high altitude, so there was none of the technical stuff to worry about. You naturally want to see caddis or mayflies on the water because they make the fish look up and let you fish a dry fly, and you might be just as naturally curious what the bugs are, but on these small freestone creeks you rarely have to copy them very closely. As far as these trout are concerned, a bug is a bug, so most days all you need for a fly pattern is something big enough for them to see and small enough to fit in their mouths. For most of the high-country season, I'll tie on a size-14 parachute dry fly and leave it on all day unless I wear it out on fish or lose it in a tree. On days when I'm prospecting hard or when the trout are pouting a little, I'll go a size smaller on the dry fly and hang a lightly weighted size-16 Hare's Ear Soft Hackle behind it on a dropper, but that's about it.

At the moment, my small-stream fly box has just over a hundred flies in it of fifteen different patterns, most in two or three sizes, but it's so rare for me to use anything but those two, I'm beginning to wonder why I carry the rest. I must still want the comfort of more flies than I need (a common crutch among fly fishers) but with just a little courage I could take another step back toward the simplicity of six or eight flies in a Prince Albert tobacco tin.

I don't know how far up the creek I went that day. It felt like three miles going in and more like a mile coming out (the difference between a hiking pace and a fishing pace), so let's split the difference and say about two miles. I caught brook trout up to ten inches or so and I reached the altitude where you start getting the occasional cutthroat.

These cutts wouldn't have been in the stream the last time I fished it. They'd since been planted in two tributaries, both separated from the creek I was on by high waterfalls. These cascades are the kind of natural barriers fish managers like because they keep the wild but exotic trout down below from working their way up into a pure cutthroat fishery.

But there's nothing to keep the cutts from working their way down except the kind of fall you'd think would kill them. Just a few weeks before, some friends and I had climbed the cascades that separate the stream I was fishing from the cutthroat water above, and it had damn near killed us. Tourists like to hike in to look at these falls and take one another's picture standing in front of them, but most don't realize that the beautiful, tall cascades they see are only about a third of what's there. It's a testament to the toughness of these fish that they could make it down that thing, even by accident, without being chewed to hamburger.

It's always fun to see cutthroats in the West because they're the original natives, but lately they've also become politically correct, so it's now all but illegal to have any misgivings about them, although I do anyway. I like the trout well enough—especially the pretty little greenback cutts that have been reintroduced into the local mountains—but the management strategy of killing off the undesirable browns, brookies and rainbows that have lived here for a century to make room for "our kind of fish" sounds a little too much like ethnic cleansing.

Anyway, I caught more and more cutts as I worked my way upstream and when I reached the mouth of the tributary I got three nice ones from a confluence pool. But then just upstream there was a six-foot plunge and I never got another cutt above that. I wondered if the same thing happened below the next creek where these fish had been planted, but that would have to wait for another trip. I'd never make it just fishing along, and I was having too much fun with the brook trout to reel in, get on high ground and make some time.

Farther on I passed a second tributary stream that was smaller than the cutthroat creek and probably fishless, and then a series of spring seeps, each hiding a deep, muddy channel under a patch of ferns—a good place to trip and fall. Beyond that the stream became noticeably smaller, but it was still plenty big enough to fish.

Later I came to a level stretch where the stream widened,

the water was shallow and riffly, and the fish were tiny. I considered turning back, but then got up on the ridge and hiked up to the next series of cascades, where the biggest trout went right back up to nine or ten inches, although they were fewer and farther between now. It was still high summer, but some of the brook trout were already in their fall spawning colors: that unlikely palette of olive, yellow, blue, red, black, white, orange and maroon that wouldn't look good on anything but a fish.

On most of these little creeks, the trout do get smaller as you go higher, and honestly, even those of us who have a soft spot for little trout in little creeks can begin to lose interest at, what? Six or seven inches? But then trout size decreases in fits and starts and there are always those spots that keep you going: the seldom-fished series of deep plunge pools or the sudden meadow stretch with deep undercuts where, against the odds, a few trout have grown big and plump and pretty and dumb. On a stream that you've either never fished before or haven't fished for too many years, one of those spots could be just over the next bench or around the next bend. You either don't know or can't remember.

You also want to keep going because you remember the fishing on most of the mountain creeks being better up high than it was down low. I think that's just because through the summer the trout really turn on in the late afternoon and that's the time of day when you're as far in as you're going to get. Still, it's a compelling illusion, especially since fishermen have a kind of predatory restlessness that we think of as curiosity. If you weren't after trout—not to mention being culturally wired for constant movement—the sights and sounds along fifty feet of stream could keep you busy all day.

• • •

I fished for the last few hours or so in one of those gentle rains that fall straight down and only dimple the water in the smooth spots behind rocks. It does rain in the high country during a drought as the mountains squeeze out the water that will never make it out to the plains, but in dry years it's often this steady drizzle instead of those sudden, hard cloudbursts. This was a rain so light I couldn't hear it over the sound of the creek except for a quiet ticking on the brim of my hat. As usual, I let myself get good and wet before I stopped fishing long enough to dig the rain slicker out of my day pack and put it on. Then I felt cold and clammy, and once again thought about turning back, but I asked myself, as a friend once asked, "You wanna be comfortable, or you wanna fish?"

I had a decent map with me, but I never bothered to look at it. (Pretty hard to get lost on a trout stream: Upstream is in, downstream is out.) And anyway, I knew where I was as much as I needed to. The cutthroat tributary had been a landmark and so had an enormous blowdown where a storm had laid the dead trunks from an old burn across the stream. Like the cutthroats, that wouldn't have been there the last time I fished the creek, but I knew roughly where the fire had been.

The downed trees had made some sweet logjam pools and I got a few good brookies from the first two, but the going finally got so sticky I had to climb halfway out of the little canyon to get around. When I finally worked my way back to the creek, I stopped to replace my dry fly because it had gotten pretty badly shredded by I don't know how many trout. I tossed the old fly in the rocks at my feet. For some reason, I don't consider that littering.

Eventually there came that moment when I was sitting on a log, a little wet, honestly tired, drinking the last of my water. It may have been raining a little harder by then or maybe I'd just stopped ignoring it. Thunder was booming down the valley and then echoing off the bare rock peaks to the west. It sounded like something very large rolling downhill, but not getting any closer.

I considered the time of day without actually looking at my pocket watch and admired the stream in the way you never quite do when you're fishing. It was narrow, lush, beautiful and familiar enough that if you'd dropped me in there blindfolded I could have told you I was on the east slope of the Colorado Rockies somewhere between Boulder Creek and the Wyoming border—all of which I greedily think of as my backyard.

It was late afternoon going on evening: time to start thinking about heading out while I could still see where I was going. I hadn't spoken a word out loud since ordering breakfast at a cafe that morning and I was not aware of missing the sound of my own voice.

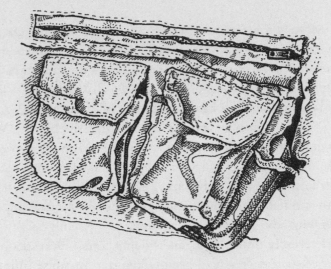

Chapter 7

I ALMOST NEVER wear a vest anymore when I'm fishing mountain streams. The few things I actually need in order to fish—leader spool, clippers, floatant and a single fly box—fit in various pants pockets, while the larger stuff— sweater, raincoat, coffeepot, water bottle, lunch—go in a small rucksack. The fishing in these creeks is pretty basic in the sense that if you can't catch the fish, it's not for lack of tools, and so the bulk of the equipment is geared for comfort or survival.

I used to wear the vest habitually. It was part of the uniform and at the time it seemed important to be noticed as a Fly Fisherman. But now I reserve the vest for tailwaters, spring creeks and faraway places where the fishing is either technical or I just don't know what to expect and therefore feel I need many pockets crammed with boxes of flies. In other words, the vest is now for special occasions, but there are enough of those that it still takes a pretty good beating every season.

More and more fly fishers are now using chest packs, butt packs and shoulder bags—all of which look unwieldy to me—but most of us still use the vest because it's a traditional item in a traditional sport. (What we call "tradition" is often just institutionalized habit, but there's still usually a reason for it.) There's a possibly apocryphal story that the late Lee Wulff invented the fishing vest years ago when he cut the sleeves off a hunting coat that had a lot of pockets. There's no proof this is true, but I believe it because I liked Lee the one time I met him and I like the story—and liking the story is the only reason why most of us believe anything.

I recently broke down and bought a new fly vest on the advice of friends who'd been telling me for some time that the old one was falling apart. I thought "falling apart" was an exaggeration, although I had to admit that the zippers on some of the pockets didn't work anymore, some of the stitching had separated and the vest had faded from khaki almost to white, with dirty gray stains where I'd habitually wiped fly floatant and fish slime from my hands a thousand times.

And there were some oddly shaped dark shadows on the back where club patches had once been sewn on. Years ago I tried my hand at being a joiner. It didn't work out because I often don't play well with others. One of those patches was from an outfit called the Outdoor Writers Association of America—a shotgun and a fly rod crossed above a typewriter. (Remember typewriters?) When I trimmed it off I saw that there was a size-12 Green Drake dry fly stuck in it. I hadn't noticed it before and couldn't remember when it happened, but it was an old pattern I hadn't used in quite a while. I could only wonder how long it had been there.

So the vest had started to look pretty funky, but not only did I not mind that, I was sort of proud of it. It takes at least a season or two to get a vest to the point where you can reach for what you want without fumbling, and more seasons yet to get it properly beat up and broken in. No one wants to be seen on the river in a brand-new vest for fear of being mistaken for a beginner.

But then on a float down the Encampment River in Wyoming, my friend Chris Schrantz pointed to a pocket that was partially worn through on the bottom and said, "You're gonna lose that fly box one of these days." A few weeks later on another river, Mike Clark pointed at yet another pocket and said, "You're about to lose whatever's in there." It was a small carbide stone for sharpening hooks and he was right: Another sixteenth of an inch on the existing hole and the stone was going into the river. This was only a few days after I'd pulled a retractor pin off because the threadbare fabric it was fastened to had finally torn away.

Chris and Mike had both kidded me about the vest before, but they were past that now and were just trying to be helpful. I figured the next step was some kind of tough-love intervention where they'd physically take the vest away from me the way you'd take the car keys from a drunk.

I'd have happily bought another vest just like the old one, but the thing was over twenty years old and you can't get them anymore because the company no longer exists. I don't know much about the ins and outs of business, but my guess is they went broke making a product that people only needed one of and that was so sturdy that even with hard use it didn't have to be replaced for two decades.

So I began to shop. I didn't like many of the vests I looked at and I was horrified at what twenty years' worth of inflation had done to the prices. More to the point, I couldn't picture any of the new vests lasting as long or becoming as comfortable as the old one.

• • •

We fishermen do tend to get sentimental about our gear (if you're not going to get all mushy about the sport, why even do it?), but we at least try to reserve that for the stuff that qualifies as durable goods, which isn't all of it by a long shot.

We all have our favorite fly patterns, but the individual flies themselves are expendable. They get broken off or chewed to pieces by hungry fish, as they should be, and for those of us who tie our own, there's always the hope that each new batch we turn out will be just a little bit better than the last.

Monofilament tippet material deteriorates with age and exposure to sunlight and should be replaced every season whether you've used it up or not. There's a brand I like, but I could change without being heartbroken if they stopped making it. I have a ritual where I throw away all my old leader spools—even if they're unused—and buy new ones every year, usually in late winter or spring when the fly shop has just gotten a fresh batch.

This is one of those small but critical things. Virtually all fishing catastrophes are caused by operator error with the possible exception of brittle tippet. But then that's operator error, too, because the operator forgot to replace it. As a friend of mine says, "Nothing is ever anyone else's fault." That's one of three mottoes to live by that I have posted in my office. The other two, also quotes from friends, are, "Have no partners" and "Never put anything up your ass that you can't get out yourself."

Fly lines wear out, too, and the sooner the better because it means you're fishing a lot. A clean new line casts better than an old dirty one and you can extend the life of a line by cleaning it once in a while, but it's still rare for a line to last through more than a season or two of hard use. I've had specialty lines last for quite a while, but the ones I use the most usually need to be replaced once a year, or turned around if they're double tapers.

I like a certain brand of floating fly line because they're good lines and, more importantly, because they haven't changed appreciably since the 1960s. There are lots of other good fly lines on the market—possibly even better ones—but many companies change their lines every couple of years, so you never quite know what you're getting, and if you really liked your old line, you can't replace it.

Bill Logan, who for years wrote the outdoor column for the *Rocky Mountain News* in Denver, once said that your line is one of your most valuable pieces of tackle and you should get the best one possible, especially since the difference in price between the best line in the world and the worst is only a few dollars. It's gotten to be a few dollars more since he wrote that, but it's still good advice.

Waders wear out, and they also change, often for the better, at least after the kinks in the latest hot new thing get worked out. I'm always slow to embrace the new technology—especially since many companies let their paying customers do their field-testing for them—but in the long run, neoprene really was better than rubberized canvas and Gore-Tex really is better than neoprene.

My current pair of Gore-Tex chest waders is the most comfortable and longest-lasting pair of waders I've ever owned. They've lasted through seven years of hard use with no pampering and some abuse, but in this seventh year I've had to go over them twice to patch what turned out to be dozens of pinhole leaks, and I still find seepers every time I go out. Those leaks are all between the back of the knees and the butt and come from sitting on the bank to think things over.

But that's not a special circumstance. Some of us sit on river-banks more than others, but we all do it.

Seven years is a good long life for a pair of waders, although for what they cost now you should be able to pass them down to your grandchildren. But high cost just seems to be part of the deal. Fly tackle is expensive by virtue of being fly tackle. It's the same principle by which food in a restaurant with linen tablecloths and snooty waiters can cost five times what it's worth.

So many of the things we use now are disposable (and fishing tackle isn't the worst of it) that most of us end up settling on a few things that seem more or less permanent out of self-defense, because we'd like to think we're more than just a quick stop between the manufacturer and the landfill. For me those few things include bamboo fly rods and hardcover books, but not fly vests.

Of course anything you've used for twenty-some years of mostly good times is bound to get to you a little, and I'm the kind who could equate the demise of an old piece of clothing with mortality itself. But luckily I'm too worried about sounding ridiculous to actually do that.

It's the hardware—rods, reels, fly boxes, landing nets, things like that—that we get attached to because they should, and often do last. Some fishermen can buy into a piece of tackle overnight, but I usually have to use something for years before I decide I really like it, and then I like it to last a while longer, if not actually forever.

Two things I've noticed over a lifetime of buying and using fishing gear is how much of it there is and how little of it floats to the top and stays there. The history of fishing tackle is a lot like the history of merchandise in general: a parade of unremarkable gizmos, punctuated here and there by true quality and durability.

For instance, most of my bamboo rods were bought used (presumably after someone else was through with them or died before they could wear them out) and some are at least as old as I am, which dates them to the mid 1940s. I take a kind of comfort in the fact that, even with hard use and the inevitable repairs, they still work about as well as they ever did and, most days, so do I.

In fact, a few of my brand loyalties have now outlasted the actual brands, which puts me in the same camp with my friend Dave Hughes, who once said, when he was asked to judge the best new tackle of the season at one of the fishing shows, "I'm not the guy to do this; all my favorite stuff is fifty years old."

I guess how you feel about the tackle industry depends on whether or not you view business in general as predatory, which is hard not to do in America today. On the other hand, even the biggest corporate fishing outfits are a few steps down the food chain from Enron and Halliburton, and the worst sin they're capable of is overspecialization. For instance, one company sells, by my count, 176 different models of fly line—one for every conceivable fish in every conceivable situation— even though a floating line and a sinker or two will get you by almost anywhere. Your native cynicism makes you wonder if the manufacturers really believe some of this gear is useful, or if they just think they can sell it, which doesn't have to be two different things, but often is.

Virtually all fishing tackle is said to have been thoroughly tested and approved by guides and other experts and some of it is, but I'm always suspicious of the claim because of an early experience. When I first started publishing regularly in the fishing magazines, I was asked to be a rod tester for a well-known tackle company. As an earnest and literal-minded Midwesterner, I thought they really wanted to know what I thought, but after two unfavorable reviews my career as a rod tester came to a sudden halt. As it turned out, they were trading free tackle for endorsements and it was embarrassing to be the one bumpkin who didn't understand that.

I'm also told by those who should know that, according to surveys, the majority of fly-fishing tackle is sold to people who spend no more than seven days a year actually fishing and who are therefore at a tremendous disadvantage. Of course the industry never comes right out and says that you can make up for lack of experience with the newest technology, and to their credit, most of the people I've met in the business will admit that. It's true that some of the gear that's for sale may make a fisherman's life a little easier, but almost none of it will help you catch a fish you wouldn't have caught anyway.

But to some extent, the fishing business sells unreasonable expectations and it works because of our cultural bias. I mean, if money can buy power, why couldn't it buy a couple of big trout? In actual fact, the way to learn how to fish is to spend lots of time on the water using as much or as little tackle as you can afford and feel comfortable with. If you have limited time, you'd be better off getting some casting lessons and practicing on the lawn now and then. Hiring a guide when you go fishing helps as long as you're willing to listen to instructions and have the fundamental skill it takes to follow them. A new rod probably won't help unless you're already an adequate caster and your old rod is a real dog.

Of course I say that as a guy with an entire room in his house dedicated to fly-tying material and fishing tackle, with the larger stuff stored out in the garage. I spent more than thirty years accumulating gear and came late to simplicity, but

I've developed a real taste for it, if only because it sounds so right when you say it out loud. For instance, when asked how to get rich, financial guru Armand Hammer once said, "Buy real estate and live a long life," which is no less true for being easier said than done.

If you truly love something, you should probably do it more than one week out of every year in the interest of mental health, but of course that would be in a perfect world. Most people who don't fish enough have perfectly good reasons—every ounce of time and money is tied up making a living, or maybe they're busting their humps trying to raise a couple of kids who, by age sixteen, will have become supremely ungrateful—but others I wonder about. There are inevitably those guys who say things like, "If I go fishing again, my wife will kill me" and I'm always astonished by that. I mean, if it's not true, why say it? And if it *is* true, why the hell did you marry her?

I finally did buy a new vest that will probably work out fine as soon as I get used to it—and it will *take* some getting used to. Like all the other vests I've seen, the design of this one is entirely too specific, so I have to deal with where someone else thinks I should put my stuff and I have to wonder about those oddly shaped pockets that nothing quite fits into. Apparently they're meant for pieces of equipment I'm unfamiliar with. (A hunting coat with four big pockets and the sleeves removed looks better all the time.) The new vest's one advantage is that it has large front pockets in roughly the same places the old one did. It was also on sale as a closeout, so it was nice and cheap.

My fly boxes fit into the new vest more or less where they did in the old one, and its loaded weight went immediately to the eight pounds or so that I'm used to, which often feels like thirty pounds at the end of the day and gives me that familiar upper backache by late afternoon. That's another reason why I shed the vest whenever possible.

Most of the other stuff went more or less where I think it belongs except the leader spools. Unbelievably, those small front pockets aren't quite big enough for four normal-sized tippet spools, let alone the larger ones for Maxima that I use for the butt sections of my hand-tied leaders. I have to wonder what fool would make a fly vest with pockets too small for leader, but then I got it cheap because it had been discontinued, so maybe I'm not the first one to wonder about that.

I did the housecleaning that seems called for when you switch stuff from one vest to another, but after over twenty years there wasn't much I could get rid of: duplicate mosquito repellent, a snarl of leader I picked up somewhere, a mysterious business card, a sandwich wrapper and something in a plastic bag that may once have been a piece of cheese.

Everything else seemed indispensable, which once again caused me to wonder why we need all that stuff. A fly fisherman from fifty years ago would wonder what it's all for. On the other hand, a modern bass fisher with a boat full of electronics and a tackle box the size of a suitcase might wonder how we get by with so little.

The new vest seems a little flimsy compared to the old one—the fabric is too thin, the zippers are too cheap—but then to those of us of a certain age, all new things look flimsy. And unfortunately it's not the regulation military khaki that fishing vests had been for at least the last few generations. It's the sort of indescribably fashionable color they'd now call "desert sage" or "misty heather." That's annoying, but as Kurt Vonnegut once said, "You can't fight progress. The best you can do is ignore it."

74

Chapter 8

THERE WERE four of us that day: Kathy and Hanno Jenson, Mike Clark and me—a little too large a group to be fishing a small mountain creek, but still a manageable number as long as no one charged out too far ahead. When that happens, the ones coming along behind don't know which pools have been fished and which have been passed by. As my late Uncle Leonard would have said, they'd be "stuck with the hind tit."

The trouble was, Mike and I *had* charged out ahead. Not on purpose; it just happened. We'd leapfrogged up the stream, catching some nice, fat little rainbows and brook trout and apparently not realizing how fast we'd been going. It finally occurred to us that it was long past time for Kathy and Hanno to have worked past us to some unfished water upstream, but we hadn't seen them for a while and there was no way they could have gone around us unnoticed in that narrow gorge.

We climbed up on a boulder that gave us a decent view downstream to the last bend and watched for a few minutes. You can't always spot people right off, but eventually you'll see movement in the trees, the color of someone's hat, the flash of a rod or a fly line snaking out across the stream. But after several minutes there was still nothing.

Mike volunteered to go back and see where they were and I was happy enough to let him. We'd only been at it for a few hours, but I'd skidded, stumbled or tripped every five steps and, frankly, I was a little whipped from constantly having to catch myself.

We were fishing through a deep gorge and the going had been a struggle. The rock walls were narrow, high and sheer. In most places you either couldn't get out at all, or you'd have to break down your rod and stuff it in your pack so you could use both hands for climbing. This was one of those places where you go in at the bottom and fish upstream to the top with no possibility of changing plans.

What passed for the bank of the stream was loose rock scree tilted at an uncomfortably steep angle, punctuated by rock piles and patches of willow, birch, dogwood and ferns that kept you from seeing where you were putting your feet. There were rafts of driftwood from years of spring floods that looked solid, but weren't. There were boulder piles that left you wondering how to get around or over, although so far there'd always been a way.

After Mike left, I fished two more small pools—missing one strike and landing a nice brook trout—and then decided I'd better stop and wait. For some reason, I was more tempted than usual to fish out ahead of everyone and I had to consciously reassert my sense of generosity by reminding myself that I wasn't alone. It took a few minutes, but I located a comfortable flat rock with a backrest, shed my pack, had a long drink of water and took a good look around.

This was an awfully pretty place in a part of the world that's renowned for its pretty places. The rock cliffs were a grayish pink color (the local sandstone with its dash of iron oxide) and they were streaked and patched with lichens shading from burnt orange to green to olive to chartreuse to yellow, and watery mineral stains tending to shades of charcoal gray. These colors would change with the light and either darken or brighten when they got wet, depending on their nature: A rusty lichen lights up like neon in the rain; a gray water stain goes black. A rock cliff is like a familiar face that you never tire of looking at because it's always recognizable, but never quite the same.

This particular sedimentary rock flakes off smooth and flat (one of the reasons it slides under your feet so easily) and I once asked a geologist friend why you never find fossils in it. He said it's because it predates life on the planet. Imagine that.

The lip of the gorge was forested in fir and spruce with the odd patch of aspen here and there, already turning yellow in August. There were a few tall, solitary spruce trees down along the creek, plus the shorter bankside deciduous growth up above the high water line, but down in the bottom it was mostly those broken, raw rocks from the size of your palm to the size of a garage, all crazily piled and skidded to a precarious stop. Long stretches of it looked like they could come loose at any second and slide into the creek, but it was more likely to be just the rock under your boot that slipped and clattered.

The stream itself was small anyway and even smaller now because of low late-summer flows combined with the ongoing drought, but there were still plenty of deep, stair-step holes caused by the steep gradient. Some fishy pools were obvious, but there were sleepers, too: narrow creases and miniature slicks here and there where a foot-long trout could make a living in a place just big enough for him to swim in a tight circle. If things went well, that fish could live for maybe four years—five tops—in the shadow of a rock older than life itself. When I'm alone in the woods I sometimes think about these things, although I rarely reach any conclusions.

This was the third dry year in a row, so the water was low and clear, and the structure of the stream was more exposed than it had been in recent memory. That was another reason why we'd decided to fish it. In a deep, narrow slot like this, the water can stay too high and fast to fly-fish until late in the summer and in a wet year you might not be able to fish it at all. But low water had opened the window a little wider and after several years of it, we were really getting a handle on the opportunities presented by fishing through the drought.

The trout were pretty much where you'd expect them to be (though they were easy to spook because of the low water and the bright sunlight) and they were fatter than what you'd expect in a high-altitude stream. This was one of those canyon waters where no appreciable runoff for three years had lengthened the growing season and just generally made day-to-day fish life a little easier. I've looked into this gorge in wet years when it was nothing but white water, spray and a dull roar. This is how the gorge was cut, but you have to wonder what the trout do when it's like that.

We'd gone in there thinking this might be a sweet spot. The stream itself is well known: Its entire course lies inside a popular national park and either roads or wide trails run along most of it. The groomed and clearly marked hiking trail that parallels part of the gorge's rim leads to a pretty waterfall that draws a good crowd most days, and then on up to some alpine lakes.

When we'd driven up that morning, the closest parking lot had been full, so we'd parked somewhere else and grabbed a free shuttle bus back up to the trailhead. There were park rangers in orange vests with 9-mm pistols on their hips directing traffic, as well as the usual percentage of the crowd who were more impatient than necessary and that vaguely familiar sense of being successfully processed.

But the gorge was off the map for most tourists and too rough for most day-hikers, who are usually after more distance and the kind of enormous vistas this country can reward you with. The view into a gorge can be spectacular, but the view out is a little claustrophobic.

As for fishermen, none of us had ever been in there and we'd never talked to anyone who had, probably because in normal years it's unfishable except for a few weeks every season. Mike and I had known about it for thirty years and figured it was about time. Kathy and Hanno were fairly new to the state and didn't have an opinion one way or the other, but they were game the way fishermen are. A hard hike to a little mountain creek? No guarantees about the fish? Okay.

It panned out the way we expected. The trout weren't shy about flies, some of them had grown to a chubby twelve or thirteen inches—about maximum size for a little stream at that altitude—and there'd been no sign of other fishermen in there. By no sign I mean no garbage; it would take a backhoe to wear a trail or leave anything like a footprint in those rocks.

You do see garbage in the more accessible parts of this park. Cans, bottles, potato-chip bags, hamburger wrappers,

Styrofoam cups, and, it must be said, plastic leader packages, snarls of monofilament, empty floatant bottles and fluorescent strike indicators that will decompose only in geologic time. What bothers me most about this is that some of the same morons who throw their trash around in national parks also vote. That alone would explain the state of American politics.

And underwear. The place isn't exactly littered with it, but you do see way more underpants lying around than you'd expect; sometimes two or three pair a day on the more well-traveled trails. The phenomenon had me baffled until a park ranger explained it. The family vacation, too many chili dogs, too much excitement, too much unaccustomed exercise. People leave skid marks in their shorts and, at a loss for anything better to do, just drop them on the trail for the rest of us to enjoy. So there you have it: Another one of life's mysteries solved.

It was one of those bright but cool late-summer days that feel a lot like fall above 9,000 feet. The rock I was lounging on was in the sun, so I was feeling pretty cozy; alternately dozing, thinking deep or at least private thoughts, and feeling blissfully alone. Mike had been gone a long time and I was just beginning to wonder where he was when I heard a faint child's voice saying, "Daddy, how did that man get down there?"

I glanced at the top of the cliff where the trail must have looped close to the edge, and a hundred feet above were a dozen tourists standing there looking at me. I didn't know what else to do, so I waved, but only the kid waved back. The adults stared at me blankly—rudely, I thought—and I began to feel like one of those interpretive exhibits you sometimes see along trails: "Aging hippies with bamboo fly rods are still sometimes seen wandering the park, although their numbers are dwindling due to loss of habitat ..."

I pulled my hat down over my eyes and pretended to sleep. When I peeked again after a few minutes, they were gone.

Some days this is the sport. You find a place where people don't go for one reason or another; then you go there and catch a few trout. It's not that you want the trout so badly or that you so desperately need them to be easier to catch or two or three inches longer than they are somewhere else. Actually, I'm not sure exactly what it is, but if fishing strikes you in a certain way, you just have to go see for yourself.

The particulars are endlessly varied, but the plot is always the same: There are some fish, usually a mix of rainbows, browns or brook trout from old plantings. There might be some cutthroats, and you desperately want those to be descendants of the old natives that have somehow held out. Now and then they are, but more likely they're from reintroductions of native fish—close, but not quite the same.

Whatever kind of trout are in the stream, a few are bigger than the rest and they seem even bigger than they really are compared to the dinks. This makes you much happier than the usual fly-fishing hype would lead you to expect, and if it happens to be right under everyone's nose, so much the better.

Daddy, how did that man get down there?

I don't know, Billy. He must be on drugs or something.

Not long after that, Mike, Kathy and Hanno showed up. They were picking their way slowly and carefully through the rocks, stumbling and skidding, but it seemed to me they were being a little more careful than usual and that Hanno was limping slightly. When they got close, I saw that Hanno's face didn't look quite right, and when they got even closer I could see that his forehead, nose and cheek looked like raw hamburger.

It turned out he'd stepped on a rock that teetered and he'd gone down in one of those falls that are so hard and sudden you think you must have been shot. He'd bashed his face pretty badly, jammed a finger and broken his bamboo fly rod in two places. The break in the butt section was caused by a basketball-sized rock that bounced down and landed on the rod, barely missing his head. The way Hanno told it, it was just a fall, but the rolling boulder suggested more of a landslide.

Mike and Kathy had cleaned the wounds as well as they could with a bandana and stream water and then gone through the rest of the drill, making sure the patient's eyes focused, that he wasn't dizzy or pale, or cold and sweaty, and checking to see if anything was broken or sprained. Then Mike, a bamboo-rod maker by trade, pushed the bamboo splinters back into place and wrapped them tightly with monofilament leader material, covering the breaks themselves and maybe an inch or two on either side. Later, in his shop, he'd redo the work, meticulously gluing the splinters back in place and covering the patches with wraps of pale yellow silk that would turn clear and all but vanish when they were coated with spar varnish. The rod would never be as good as new, but it would be good enough to use. Mike pointed out that if the same thing had happened to a graphite rod, it would have been done for. That seemed to please him immensely.

The idea of breaking a bamboo fly rod makes most fishermen's blood run cold, but then when it happens, it's suddenly not the end of the world—especially when you're stunned and bleeding and a long way from the nearest road. Years ago an old (and I mean elderly) friend of mine took a bad fall in a stream canyon very much like this one. He was alone and miles from help in rough country. He tripped, fell and hit so hard he momentarily blacked out. He told me about it a few days later. He said that when he came to, his first thought was, Please God, if anything is broken, let it be the rod.

The splice Mike did on the stream wasn't that pretty and the slick monofilament didn't want to hold the whip finish, but the rod held together well enough to be fished for the rest of the afternoon. Hanno asked if anyone had some aspirin and no one did, but he held together well enough, too.

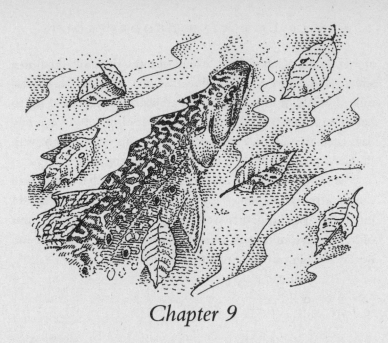

Chapter 9

I WANT TO tell you about a particular brook trout I caught on my last trip to Labrador because I have to tell someone. I was fishing out of Three Rivers Lodge on the Woods River with A.K. and Jim Babb, and although it was only our third day out, we'd already done way better than we'd expected. In the first two days, we'd each caught over a dozen brook trout between three and six pounds, plus a few that were exceptional even for Labrador. The day before, A.K. had landed an eight-pounder, and that evening he and I caught almost identical nine-pounders from the same spot—all on dry flies and all without doing anything special. The guide pointed to some rapids, said, "Fish there," and we did.

It sometimes amazes me the lengths to which my friends and I will now and then go just to catch some fish, but then something like that happens and it all becomes clear.

In three previous trips to Labrador, fishing parts of a different drainage, A.K. and I had landed lots of brook trout over five pounds and a few in the neighborhood of seven, but although we'd heard stories about these eight- and nine-pounders, I think we only half believed they existed and only half cared. It's an article of faith among fishermen that there are always bigger fish in the water than the ones you're catching, although if that makes you look askance at the five-pounder in your net for even a second, you risk a life of frustration. But then there we were again, in a new part of the same country, and there were the fish that even the locals would call big, as if it happened all the time.

The size of the fish was probably a function of the area having been fished for only the last three years by a relative handful of sports, and the fact that the management hadn't succumbed to that endless-bounty-of-the-wilderness crap. The places where A.K. and I had fished for brook trout in Labrador before had been in operation for decades and they had what looked like a pretty enlightened policy. It was catch and release on the brook trout with the one exception that you could keep a single fish as a trophy.

That seemed reasonable, but then the brook trout aren't packed into these waters like eight-inch brookies in a beaver pond, and the largest are also the oldest and rarest. Even with only a few trophies being killed every season, the average size had declined slightly over the years. And although the remaining fish were astonishingly large to almost anyone from almost anywhere, the population had nonetheless been culled from the top down by sports and management who thought they were being responsible. Fish hoggery seemed to be prohibited by the camp policies, but then fish hogs are endlessly inventive and patient. At one camp there was the story of a regular client who, over the years, had killed and mounted four brook trout weighing eight pounds or more. Everyone agreed this had happened. No one could say why.

Apparently none of that had been lost on the people at Three Rivers. When we all arrived at the lodge and sat down over coffee for the inevitable orientation meeting, it was mercifully short. Robin Reeve, the owner, said there were only two rules: 1) If your guide tells you to do something, do it and argue later. And 2) No one ever kills a brook trout for any reason. Not ever, period.

The exact location of Labrador doesn't spring immediately to mind for most people. For the record, it's part of the northeasternmost mainland province of Canada, on the Atlantic Coast northwest of the island of Newfoundland. It's possible to learn very little about the politics and culture when you're in a place like this. For one thing, you're only there for a week or so and you spend most of your waking hours fishing, traveling to fish or talking about fishing. For another, wise guides don't air their dirty laundry to the clients, most of whom have a pile of laundry at home that they've gone fishing to forget about.

Still, I thought I detected a slight sore spot. On all but the newest maps, you'll see Labrador listed as part of Newfoundland or, worse yet, as "the mainland territory" of that province, but the people who live there don't seem to consider themselves to be in anyone's territory besides their own, thank you very much. (In recognition of this, the province was officially renamed "Newfoundland and Labrador" in 2001.) In Labrador, Newfoundland is referred to as "The Rock."

Labrador is an enormous, roadless place that stretches from the last subarctic spruce/fir forests up to the tundra in the direction of the Arctic Circle. It's a country of huge lakes and rivers where there isn't enough dry land to travel by foot and where direct water routes of any length are almost unknown, so it can take all day in a motorized canoe to go ten miles as the crow flies—given a break from the weather, of course. Before the advent of the float plane, travel as we modern fishermen know it was all but impossible. The native people traveled in winter, when the lakes and bogs were frozen hard and you could go in a more or less straight line—again, given a break from weather.

We were told it had been dry there recently and the water levels were down a little from previous years. I couldn't tell. Coming from a semiarid climate in the grip of drought, this looked to me like the place where all the freshwater in the world was born. It was like being in heaven, notwithstanding clouds of mosquitoes, black flies and the big caribou flies known locally as "stouts" that attacked like miniature winged rottweilers. On a normal summer trip to Labrador, you'll smear on enough 100 percent Deet to permanently change your genetic code, and of course the worst days for bugs—overcast, still, with temperatures in the mid 60s—are the best for fishing.

The afternoon of that third day, we ended up on the Eagle River, so-called because a pair of bald eagles are known to nest along its banks. Since the camp had been open for only a few years, it wouldn't have been too long ago that this place was referred to as "that river over there with the eagle nest," and then in the normal evolutionary path of place-names, that would have been immediately shortened to "Eagle River." The eagles themselves hadn't been seen that year, but the nest was still there and in good condition, and there was something deeply romantic about being in a place where the names of things were that fresh.

The Eagle is typical of northern rivers in that it's wide and rocky and carries a good head of water, but it's unusual because it runs for a good long way as recognizable flowing water. What they call rivers up there are usually chains of lakes covering hundreds of square miles strung together by short rapids that are often hours apart by canoe, or closer by float plane.

You go to the rapids because that's where the fish stack up. The rapids are numbered instead of named, and although you might prefer a little more frontier poetry, the numbers do place them neatly in order of distance from the camp. Those two big brook trout the night before came from a side channel running into Fifth Rapids that's known as Little Fifth.

The Eagle is largely unwadable and wide enough so that in many places two good fly casters working from opposite banks would still leave a third of it untouched. The water is clear but tea-colored from all the peat and spruce needles, and the banks are jumbled rock and brush with deep holes and sudden, black drop-offs. This far north, the last ice-age glaciers have only recently melted back and the land hasn't had a chance to soften as it has farther south. Everything is still raw and it reminds me of the high country in the Rocky Mountains except that the streams are bigger and the land is flat.

The surrounding forest is short and a little on the scraggly side because it's close to the northern tree line and the growing season is brief. (When you cut a black spruce for firewood, you find growth rings as tight as the grooves on a vinyl record.) The forest floor is rock and bog almost uniformly covered with caribou moss, which is slippery even when it's dry. The guides stroll across it as if it were a paved sidewalk. The rest of us skid and stumble and fall behind.

The three of us had spread out along the river and our guide, Doug, happened to be with me, either because he thought I might catch a fish, or because I looked like I needed help. You can never tell with guides.

I was fishing the big plunge pools along the right bank with a size-4 weighted Muddler Minnow. I would roll-cast the streamer to the bubbly water at the head of the pool, mend it upstream a few times to let it sink and then twitch it out on the near side where the current slowed. I caught a pretty, three-pound brook trout and then a nice ten-pound lake trout that Doug landed with his long-handled net.

He took a snapshot of me with the laker and then headed off at a fast walk to see how A.K. and Jim were doing. (A guide with three sports strung out of sight along a rough river can cover a lot of ground in an afternoon.)

Ten minutes later, I'd crashed through enough brush and teetered out on enough boulders to reach the next plunge pool, and on my first cast I hooked a heavy fish. It wallowed in the pool for a few seconds and I got a good enough look to see that it was a very large brook trout. Then the fish got into the current and ran downstream into the next pool. I tried to stop him, but this was a heavy one and there *was* no stopping him.

This is where you're supposed to follow your fish downstream, but that couldn't happen. I was already perched on the last downstream rock, with a bottomless hole below me and an impenetrable tangle of spruce and alders on the bank.

I played the fish in the next pool—thirty or forty feet away—and when he started to give a little, I tried to work him back upstream in the current. It didn't work. He was too heavy; the current was too strong. All it took was a little flip of his tail and he was peeling line down into the pool again. I looked around for Doug and his net, but he was long gone. I thought about screaming for help, but I don't know if I actually did or not. I might have been too embarrassed.

I tried two more times to work the fish back up current, but he just wouldn't come and I felt that I was past the outside limit of my tackle: a size-4 fly, 2x tippet and a nearly eighty-year-old H. L. Leonard 6-weight bamboo fly rod.

Okay, I know that wasn't the right rod for this river, but that morning when we left camp we were headed for Victoria Creek, which Doug had named for his daughter. He said it was a pretty little thing where we'd probably catch only small fish and it sounded like a good place to air out the old Leonard.

Catching little brook trout in Labrador is strangely comforting. It's something you should do after a couple of big fish days to lower the pitch and regain some perspective. But then later that day, on the way back to camp, we decided to stop and put in a few hours on the Eagle, and the old rod was the only one I had with me. What would you have done?

Anyway, at this point the fight had begun to look hopeless. The trout was tired, so was I, we were still thirty feet apart and we seemed to have reached a stalemate. I remember thinking that a better man than me would admit defeat and break the fish off, but it would have *taken* a better man.

Finally, I hooked the toe of my boot in an alder root, leaned as far out over the pool as I could and dragged the fish unceremoniously up the far side of the rip where the current was just a little bit slower. Apparently I'd decided this was as good a moment as any to break a fine old rod, lose the fish or both.

As I was hauling the fish back up into my pool, I tried to point the rod at him to keep the strain in the butt—at least I was thinking clearly about that—but to get him over to my side of the fast current without losing him downstream again, I had to bend the old rod nearly double with a trembling forearm.

I don't know if I winced at the time, but I wince now remembering it. Anyone who knows bamboo rods will tell you to never, *ever* do that. If the fish had so much as wiggled, he'd have snapped the rod like a twig.

I didn't land the fish all that gracefully, but I landed it as well as I could without a net. It was huge.

The nine-pound brook trout I'd caught the night before—with the guide there to verify the weight—was still fresh in my mind. This one was easily that long, measured clumsily against the rod's old-fashioned intermediate wraps, and it seemed wider across the back, deeper in the gut and heavier. Whether it actually *was* heavier or just seemed that way is, I suppose, up for grabs at a moment like that. But it was clearly the biggest brook trout I'd ever caught or seen or even imagined. That much I know for sure.

I took a good, long look at the fish as I cradled it in the water to revive it. I wished I could get to my camera for even a clumsy, one-handed shot, but it was out of reach in the back of my vest and I didn't have a free hand. I wished I had a scale, but I didn't. I wished for a witness, but there was no one around. Just for an instant, I pined for the time when you could feel okay about killing a fish like this and dragging it triumphantly back to camp, but those days are long gone—as they should be.

I tried my best to burn the whole thing into memory just the way it was at that moment: the rocks, alders, pool, rod and fish—a still life with brook trout. When the fish had recovered enough to give a good wiggle, I let it go. It swam deliberately down into the slow eye of the plunge pool until I couldn't see it anymore, although I kept looking for a long time.

I thought, Ten pounds. Then I took a deep breath and thought, More likely nine and a half and I should probably say nine pounds to be honest—or at least to be believed without some kind of verification. (A brook trout weighing ten pounds would be within ounces of the fly-rod world record.) It had been one of those moments you spend a lifetime of fishing for, but then goes by way too fast. The fish had been gone for two minutes and already I was beginning to wonder if any of this had actually happened.

I sat on the rock for a while swatting mosquitoes and trying to have profound thoughts because that's what you're supposed to do at a time like that. I managed to let my heartbeat and my breathing slow down to where I thought I could stand up without fainting, and then I was asking myself, Is this a story I should never tell?

Think about it: The brook trout of a lifetime caught when you're alone? A guess at size by a guy who's seen precious few trout anywhere near that big? I'd worry about sounding hysterical. My friends would be generous, but skeptical in spite of themselves. Later they might carefully say that I "claimed" to have caught a ten-pound brook trout, but of course there was no one else there to see it.

If I kept this to myself, I'd never have to see that look of doubt in anyone's eyes. I mean, it wouldn't be the first time a fisherman all by himself on a remote river had freaked out and guessed the weight of a fish a little high. If I never told, I'd never have to convince anyone and I could stay convinced myself. It would be a secret I could take out and admire every now and then. Someone might ask what I was smiling about and I could say, "Oh, nothing."

But this was a good one and I had to wonder—not for the first time—if I fish for the pure sake of the fishing or for the stories. When I'd degenerated into this kind of navel-gazing in the past, it had always come down to the same thing: I try to write the stories as well as I can because it's my chosen craft, but also because I know they'll eventually replace the actual memories. You write what you remember and then remember what's written down. Never telling about that enormous brook trout could show me, once and for all, why I fish—if I really wanted to know.

I scrambled up the bank into the trees and headed down a convenient caribou trail to where the canoe was beached at the mouth of the river. It was early yet and no one would be there for a while, but I was done fishing and needed the time alone to collect myself. Of course I'd tell the story; once in the boat and then again back in camp. I was rehearsing it already, looking for just the right note of understated certainty.

When I thought to stop and sight down my rod, I saw it had taken a bad set. It was severely bent from the midsection out through the tip, as if it were still playing the fish that had already been landed and released. This is the kind of thing a good bamboo-rod maker can fix, although not completely. He'll make it straight again, but the rod will never be quite the same. A little bit of the life will have been fished out of it, not unlike its owner.

Still, I was glad it had happened because it would be the only proof I had to offer.

Chapter 10

IWAS HAVING breakfast at Andrea's Cafe—sitting alone with my nose in a book—when Mike Price walked in, sat down at the table and ordered coffee. I hadn't seen him in a long time, but that wasn't unusual. Mike is the kind who'll vanish for weeks or even months at a time and then reappear pretty much without comment, as if he saw you just yesterday.

I said, "It's been a while."

He said, "Huh?"

We had breakfast together and the talk was predictable: where we'd been fishing, where our friends had been fishing and where we might go again soon. It was late summer and everything was still wide open—or almost everything, there being a few exceptions for what was beginning to look like chronic low water—but it wouldn't be long before the possibilities would begin to shut down for the season. Beginning in the high country and then working on down to the foothills and plains, the fishing ends in sequence, like a janitor turning off the lights and locking the doors on the last day of school.

This is perfectly natural and you get used to it, although in the third year of drought there's the added poignancy of wondering if this will be the winter when one or more of your favorite streams will finally get low enough to freeze right to the bottom as anchor ice and kill all the fish.

Over our second cups of coffee, Mike told me about a couple of good-sized brown trout he'd been trying to catch for most of the summer. In fact he'd told me about these same fish before, sometimes in excruciating detail. Apparently they'd really gotten under his skin.

These weren't huge trout—they were maybe seventeen or eighteen inches long—but they were big for the water they were in and they were in a difficult spot. They were also unusually shy, which is odd because they're in a private stretch of stream that isn't fished very hard—or at least isn't supposed to be. But then trout are suspicious by nature, so maybe they were just exercising the native caution that let them get big in the first place.

Mike said he'd screwed up the difficult cast often enough, but even when he thought he got it right and had tied on what had to be the right fly, the fish simply stopped rising and sank to the bottom to sulk. (I don't know about you, but I actually prefer it when a fish bolts in terror, as if I were a real threat instead of just an annoyance.) Anyway, he'd caught a smaller trout from the same pool a couple of times, but the big boys just didn't seem interested. He started describing the pool and the cast again and then said, "Well, hell, let's just go look at it."

It took us ten minutes to drive out to the spot, which wasn't quite where I'd pictured it from his earlier descriptions.

Then we got up on the high bank that would let us spot the fish without spooking them. Mike had this all worked out. The top of the knoll where we were standing was pounded almost bare, a sign that he'd been up there many times studying the situation.

The sun was bright, the water was low and clear and there was no wind, so the visibility was near perfect. Mike went into the usual drill: "Okay, see that slot a few feet out from the far bank? Now, just down from the bridge, see that white thing on the bottom? They're almost side by side about two feet straight above that." It was one of those deals where you can't see them at all, and then you can see them plain as day: two brown trout, hugging the bottom and almost motionless, one about seventeen inches long, the other just a little longer and a little wider across the back. There was also a fourteen- or fifteen-inch brown ahead of them. That was the one Mike had caught.

The white thing on the bottom turned out to be a china dinner plate. I'm always amazed at the unlikely crap that can end up in a trout stream, although so far nothing has topped the boom box I found last year in a little brook-trout creek in Rocky Mountain National Park. I could only wonder about the story behind that, although I thought it must have involved some restraint. When I'm out in the woods, my first urge isn't to drown the loud radio, but the dimwit who's playing it.

Anyway, the problem was obvious. The upstream cast would have to be a long one with a severe and accurate left hook, and it would have to be a horizontal sidearm cast that flipped the leader up under the low bridge. It would be plenty hard enough with an unobstructed back cast, but the whole bank behind where you'd have to stand was crowded

with willows. I tried to picture the sidearm forward cast together with the roll or steeple back cast it would take to keep
your line out of the bushes. Offhand, I couldn't see how you'd
manage it.

I could see how these fish would be skittish, though. The
pool was wide and slow and the water was glassy. The fish
were in a small current seam that ran down the slot, but in
late summer flows it was nothing more than a loose string of
bubbles. Even earlier in the year when the water is higher,
there wouldn't be enough current to cover anything but the
perfect cast and drift.

Mike was grinning proudly, as if he'd arranged all this as a
practical joke and I'd fallen for it.

This is the kind of spot that can keep you coming back off
and on for weeks or months. Pure persistence could do it.
Give them enough chances and maybe one of these fish
would make a mistake. Or maybe one day you'd hit the cos-
mic hatch. If there are enough insects on the water, trout will
sometimes feed so eagerly that they'll lose some of their caution. Not all of it by a long shot, but possibly just enough.
Then again, this is a small freestone creek, not the kind of
water that normally pumps out blanket hatches.

You might be able to change tactics entirely by coming
back in the dead of a moonless night and fishing a size-2
mouse fly through the pool. Larger brown trout are known to
get nocturnal and vicious, and even at seventeen or eighteen
inches they can begin to tackle some pretty large prey.

Mike shrugged and said he'd thought of that, but it didn't
seem to interest him very much. It's not that a mouse after
dark would amount to cheating; I think he'd just come to
picture this as a daytime, dry-fly problem where one day you
just make the perfect cast, either because you've been practic-

ing or just from sheer perseverance. It would only have to happen once.

I remember a story about a high school basketball player. I don't remember his name or what team he played for, but the film clip was all over the TV news for a few nights. This kid recovered the ball under the opposing team's basket and, with the score tied and only two or three seconds left in the game, he lofted it the length of the court, made the basket and won the game.

I understand that's not how the sport is usually played, but it only had to work that one time; it did and the kid's teammates carried him off the court on their shoulders.

Catching one of those brown trout on a dry fly would be a little like that, only without the screaming fans or the airtime. When and if Mike pulls it off, he'll be momentarily tempted to kill the fish as proof, but he probably won't. His friends will believe him, and if we don't it will be our problem.

My guess is Mike will get one of those trout sooner or later, if only because they're so handy. They're ten minutes from the cafe; ten minutes in the other direction from where he lives. He can wait out the right weather and stream flow and hatches; he can stop and check on them going to and from work or fishing and try that cast again every time he catches them rising. Or maybe he'll finally see that there's another way to do it that could work. Naturally, Mike carries a rod, reel and fly box in his car at all times.

Catching certain fish not only takes skill, but also a kind of sublime patience, although you often don't have that kind of luxury. Most of the apparently uncatchable fish I've located were on trips that had their own momentum. Chances are I traveled some distance to get to the river and there was a more or less fixed time to leave, so I wanted to cover some water and catch a few. I'd give a hard fish my best shot, screw it up as often as not, then shrug and move on.

But now and then you just get stuck in spite of yourself. I remember a great big rainbow on the South Platte River a few years ago. He was in a stretch of pocket water, in a four-foot-deep plunge pool, tight behind a rock with fast currents parting around on both sides and a deep, dead current eye in the middle. I won't guess at his size now, years later, but he was one of the bruisers you'd sometimes see down there: a big trout even for a river that was famous for big trout.

I tried half a dozen different nymph patterns and ended up with a clumsy, two-inch-long string of split shot on my leader to sink the fly deep enough in the current. This was a spot that defied standard nymphing technique and the fish had gotten big because he was in the perfect place—or maybe he'd taken over the place as a reward for getting that big. Anyway, I either never got the drift right or never used the right fly and I would have had to do both simultaneously. This is a heavily fished catch-and-release river and a trout that had gotten to that size would have seen it all.

The fish kept feeding the whole time, slipping lazily back and forth to pick off nymphs. Now and then I could see the white flash as he opened his mouth. So at least there was that. Whatever else I did wrong, I didn't spook him.

Finally the guy I was fishing with wandered back downstream and said, "Jeez, you still here?" When I checked my watch I saw that I'd been standing in one spot for two hours. I also noticed that my feet were numb as stones.

My friend said he'd caught fourteen fish on dry flies. I said I'd failed to catch this one, but it was a big mother. He waded up beside me, peered silently into the pool for a minute and said, "No shit."

• • •

Once some friends and I were on a river in Oregon fishing for redside trout, simply because none of us had ever caught one before. These things are a variety of coastal rainbow, but they're a distinct subspecies and you naturally want to see the difference as well as add a new fish to your life list. They're also a big deal in the regions where they live. For instance, the high school football team in the last little town we drove through is known as the Fighting Redsides—a refreshing break from the usual Cougars and Trojans.

We found some feeding fish that were easy to spot from thirty feet above by walking an old railroad bed, now the rough dirt road we'd driven in on. Some smaller eight- to ten-inch trout were nymphing out in the main current, but the bigger ones were tucked into back eddies in jumbled bankside rocks, tight to the overhanging brush. In these sheltered, shady spots you could sometimes see fish rising lazily to sip mayfly duns from the surface. This is what you'd traveled hundreds of miles for, although you hadn't imagined it being quite this difficult.

You'd spot a fish, tuck your rod under your arm and watch like a cat, doing nothing until it became clear what to do. (Novelist Craig Nova once said of his education as a fisherman, "Watching was my Harvard and my Yale.") You'd be picturing where you could scrabble down the steep, loose-rock bank, where you'd have to stand, how to snake the cast under the inevitable overhanging bush, how the line would have to lie on the braided currents so the fly would go where it had to and drift naturally, and incidentally guessing at what particular fly it would have to be.

You'd wonder if this trout was actually beyond the physical limits of the tackle, or just out of your league, and that fleeting thought would rattle your confidence. You might glance longingly at the smaller trout playing in the easier, more open water, but you'd want the big one for reasons probably dating back to prehistory, when a big fish was simply more food than a little one.

There's one spot I remember perfectly. Half a dozen tongues of current eddied in from the river at different speeds and piled back upstream. The bank was steep enough to lean on while standing nearly straight and there were waist-high tangles of wild rosebushes all along it. A nice big redside was facing downstream inches from the bank, sipping mayflies under an overhanging rosebush. This was a beautiful tall shrub completely covered with dark pink, sweet-smelling blooms and it was clutching no less than twelve feet of my fly line in its thousands of miniature thorns. It had taken me ten minutes to visualize my approach, then get into position and make a cast that was really only about three inches too close to that fucking bush.

I felt a tantrum coming on and fought it back. This is like the moment when the housefly you've been trying to swat for the last fifteen minutes finally lands on Grandma's Ming vase and a realization comes upon you suddenly—if at all. With the cast blown and your line hopelessly tangled, the trout rises again and turns just enough to show you his name-sake red sides.

And then once I was fishing some beaver ponds in a national park with my friend Paul. Paul has fished all over the place and regularly catches the big ones, but he said there was noth-ing he'd rather do than noodle some little brookies out of beaver ponds, which is what makes him a kindred soul.

We had crashed through the brush-choked beaver meadow for an hour, wading the pond edges and old channels because you couldn't go three feet on land. At one point we surprised some large animal that we never saw—probably an elk, possibly a bear—that careened off snapping branches and small trees in its wake. We both froze and our eyes went wide in the second it took to realize that whatever this was, it was terrified of us and was running for its life.

We got a few small brookies here and there in the ponds themselves and the channels connecting them, and finally came to the big, deep pond I knew was in there, but wasn't sure I could locate. Paul worked his way around to the inlet and I dropped back to look at the channel below the beaver dam.

When I loomed up over the water, some small brook trout flushed close in and darted under the cut bank at my feet. I briefly wondered why you always have to come in at the wrong spot, and then scanned farther up the channel. There were two more trout holding in a slow, deep bend, suspended inches off the silt bottom under three feet of painfully clear, smooth water. The sun was high and bright, so I saw the dark shadows of the trout first, and then the fish themselves. The smaller of the two was around a foot long—a very respectable brookie—but the big one was a good fifteen or sixteen inches. In the small scale of the four-foot-wide channel, he looked more like a tarpon than a brook trout.

I made a pretty nice cast; it's just that there was no way this could have worked out. The sun was bright, the water was clear and the current was so smooth and slow it was almost still. I laid the line as gently as I could against the right bank and hooked the fly to the left, where it landed gently three feet above the fish and right in line with them. It all happened quickly, but I think both fish saw the shadow of the line in the air and were gone by the time the fly lit on the water. I didn't even see where they went. There were just two boils of gray silt where the trout had been. The shadow of the line on the bottom looked as big as a cable.

I can't say I was heartbroken. You get over these small losses the way a lizard grows a new tail, and you end up remembering the great uncaught fish as vividly as you do the caught ones—and just as fondly, too, because there's a part of every fisherman that roots for the fish.

On the way out, we came to a smaller pond with two sets of tracks crossing the mud in the shallow end, one made by an elk, the other by a fisherman in waders. Clearly these two had come along at different times and crossed at the same place because that was where you'd cross, but I couldn't shake the mental picture of a man and an elk strolling side by side across a beaver pond.

If you get out enough, odds are you'll see your share of easy fishing, and it can begin to seem entirely reasonable that you can tie a few bits of fuzz to a hook and fool a trout (a pretty low order of creature, after all) into thinking it's a real bug. But then there are other times when the whole concept of fly-fishing begins to look like a pretty far-fetched idea. Of course this is just the universal karma of the predator. I read once where the average mountain lion attacks eight to ten mule deer before he actually brings one down and gets a meal. Who are we to expect to do better than that?

Still, you *do* get better with time and experience. Gradually, some of those impossible fish become just difficult, and when you try hard or have a good day you manage to hook and land some of the difficult ones. It takes a little bit of skill and native intelligence and lots of time on the water, but after failing to catch several dozen fish in vaguely similar spots—al-

ways for reasons that become painfully obvious afterward—
you try the one thing you never tried before because it's all
you have left. Maybe it's a complicated and brilliantly exe-
cuted cast, or maybe it's just a matter of wading upstream a
little for a better angle. Whatever. If it works, you think you'll
never forget it.

Sometimes when I'm studying a difficult fish, trying to figure out what to do, I'll get an unshakable feeling of déjà vu.
It's as if I once caught this very fish in this exact spot before,
and I'm right on the verge of remembering how the hell I
did it. Maybe it really is a memory—life gets long and there's
too much to recall clearly—or maybe it just means I'm beginning to get an idea.

Good fishing is like good drama. As someone in the movie
business once said, "In act one, you put your guy up a tree, in
act two you put him farther up the tree, and in act three you
get him down." Which is to say, I enjoy fishing for difficult
fish, although I enjoy it more when I finally manage to catch
one. When I don't, I learn for the millionth time to let go of
regret because it's pointless. The way things are is the only
way they could have been.

And, as I said, sometimes a fish will just make a mistake—and
I mean a bigger mistake than a caught fish usually makes. This
isn't something you can count on, but it does happen. The fly
is dragging badly in the current and, now that you think
about it, it's probably even the wrong pattern; but the fish eats
it anyway, sometimes so viciously you couldn't get it away
from him if you tried. We humans aren't the only ones who
are prone to periodic fits of stupidity.

There are also those times when everything clicks for no
apparent reason, as if all your molecules have momentarily

aligned, and you're temporarily better than you've ever been. It's not that your skills have improved, but that you're fishing with perfect clarity, within your limited means, entirely in the present tense, and the trout wag their tails and come to you like puppies. You wonder why it can't always be like this, even though the reason is obvious: You can't always forget that the region you love seems to be permanently drying up, or that you often have trouble making a living, or that your country's foreign policy makes you want to crawl backward out of your own skin. The fact is, you probably always know how to catch the fish, but you have to get out of your own way to do it. I notice this constantly in my own fishing. I actually *do* have all the answers, it's just that implementation is often a problem.

Oddly enough, I've seen inspired fishing happen in the wake of a failed business deal. A guy launches one of those brilliantly obvious schemes that somehow no one has thought of yet and that can't possibly miss. Three years later he's bankrupt, unemployed and divorced and he's out trout fishing. (It's a cheap sport when you do it near home and already own the tackle.) The wife and the money both left town a year ago, and although things might have gone differently, they didn't. Now he's doing nothing more complicated than renewing his faith in the unlikely, and for reasons beyond ordinary understanding, a guy like this can fish brilliantly.

But whether it's a brilliant job of fishing or just dumb luck, you'll now and then pull one off that you can't tell anyone about because it would sound too perfect and they'd have to assume you made most of it up. But whatever anyone thinks, you'll have just done something you once thought was impossible, and that may be the whole point of going fishing.

● ● ●

So Mike and I stood on the top of that knoll for a while watching those two brown trout. Now and then one of them would paddle a fin, but essentially they hadn't moved. Not only were they not feeding, they didn't even seem conscious, and I caught myself wondering if fish sleep in any way that we'd recognize. Mike said, "Feel free to try 'em sometime if you want to."

I thought about it—I'm still thinking about it—but I'll probably leave them alone. For one thing, it's unlikely that I'd be able to catch a fish that Mike can't get. For another, he'd waited to show them to me until late in a dry year, when the current had gotten so low and slow that getting a good cast over them really would be impossible. And anyway, he's enjoying his frustration too much for me to intrude.

Chapter 11

VINCE AND I had spent part of the day halfheartedly fishing a small freestone stream in the foothills of Wyoming's Laramie Mountains, and we hadn't done well. This is normally a fine little creek with browns and rainbows that are bigger than you'd expect from such small water. It's never entirely clear what makes one stream better than another, but this one is hard to find and difficult to reach, so it gets very little fishing pressure. There are also more grasshoppers along the creek than I've ever seen anywhere, and trout are known to love hoppers and to grow big on them when there's a large, regular supply. It probably goes without saying that between late June and the first hard frost, you only need one fly pattern. This is one of those pretty little secrets that can be your reward for living attentively in an interesting bioregion.

But by the time we got there this last time, it was the third straight year of drought and the stream was lower than I've ever seen it; low enough that the usual low-water mark was now serving as the high-water mark and some familiar spots were almost unrecognizable. The water was still clear and cool; there just wasn't much of it, and it had apparently been like that for a while. For instance, the big brown spiders that live there and that have a taste for aquatic insects had built their webs within inches of the current surface, spun between rocks that hadn't been dry in decades.

We hadn't fished this creek all season because we'd heard it was low and fishing poorly, but we made the drive north in early September to check it out for ourselves. We were worried about it in the proprietary way fishermen have with all trout streams and their favorites in particular.

We did fish for a while, but after missing a few strikes, landing one small brown and spooking a few other trout well beyond casting range, we reeled in and just hiked upstream, keeping our walking sticks ahead of us so as not to step on a rattlesnake and trying to spot fish. We didn't see many and we wondered what that meant. Water that gets low enough or warm enough can certainly kill trout, and since the big ones need deeper water to survive, they're the ones that go first. On the other hand, trout have an astonishing capacity to hide, even in what you'd think of as plain sight. I've seen a dozen streams I'd have sworn didn't have a fish in them, only to come back in a different flow or during a hatch to find hundreds of trout rising. It became obvious that this was one of those all-too-common exercises where you finally decide to go see for yourself, and then can't be sure what you're seeing.

Halfway up the canyon there's an old abandoned cabin with a still-functioning water pump outside. This is roughly at the midpoint, and from there you can go on up another mile and a half to an upper trail or hike out there on what's left of the dirt road leading to the cabin. But either way, you get a drink from the pump because it usually runs cold, clear and potable. This time it ran lukewarm and silty after entirely too many cranks of the handle, so we stayed thirsty as we walked the road back to the truck.

During the drought, some of my friends and I had gotten almost smug about beating the conditions by fishing in the high country, hitting the controlled tailwaters now and then and sometimes traveling to places like Labrador and Maine, where there was plenty of water, if not actually too much. But late in this third season, we'd begun to see not just low flows, but some undeniably shrunken streams, although the one we'd just walked along was the first that actually seemed too far gone to fish.

Not unexpectedly, the only trout fishery that had actually been lost that year was a man-made affair. A reservoir up in South Park had been drained dry to fill another reservoir farther downstream so that people in the Denver suburbs could continue to water their ridiculous bluegrass lawns. As the water dropped, the Division of Wildlife invited fishermen to come up and kill all the trout they could catch in what they euphemistically called a "recovery operation."

I saw some of those guys interviewed on TV one night. The reporter—and I use the term loosely—obviously went up there to do a lighthearted piece. I mean, who would be happier than a fisherman who could kill all the fish in the lake if he wanted to? But the fishermen the reporter talked to seemed sad and a little embarrassed, while the talking head seemed annoyed to have reality intrude on his preconceived idea. The lead for the story had been, "Good News for Fishermen."

Vince and I spent that night in a cheap motel out on the interstate, and the next morning, over breakfast and a map, we hatched a plot that would take us through the Laramie

Mountains and across a high basin to a rich prairie lake that was said to have some big rainbows and brook trout in it. (Small lakes and ranch reservoirs can be a better bet in a drought than small streams, simply because there's more water in one place.) There was no direct route, just a bunch of connecting dotted red lines that, according to the legend on that particular map, designated "Unimproved Roads, Trails or Old Railroad Grades."

The lake itself wasn't actually on the map (which we took as a hopeful sign) but we knew where it was supposed to be and had some scribbled directions from someone Vince knew. We also had Vince's four-wheel-drive pickup with thirty-some gallons of gas in its saddle tanks, some sandwiches, a thermos of coffee, the map and a compass. Vince would drive. I'd navigate. Piece of cake.

It took us an hour and two dead ends before we located what looked like a dirt county road that would let us go west as far as the next basin. "At least this one has a name," Vince said as he turned onto it.

I said, "The ones we just turned around on had names, too."

We were a little less confident than we'd been over bacon and eggs, but the road tended in roughly the right direction, rose gradually into some sparsely forested hills and then dropped into a high, flat basin ringed with mountains. Most importantly, it didn't end abruptly at a locked gate with a threatening sign, as the others had.

It was a good twenty miles to the first crossroad. There was a sign, but the road signs in that part of Wyoming were made of painted plywood before the more durable metal ones became common a few generations ago. During that time, constant wind and grit, wetting and drying and freezing and thawing have rendered them all but unreadable. Not that it would matter much. You wouldn't see half a dozen people a year on this road who didn't already know where they were.

We got out of the truck and stared at the sign from a foot away. "It says 'something c-o-u- . . .'—probably 'county'—but is that a 6, a 9, or an 8?"

"Well, there's a Road 6 on the map, but no 8 or 9. You sure that looks like a 6?"

"Pretty sure. And it goes north like it should. This has to be it."

We went on like that for another forty miles or so. Luckily, there weren't many intersections and there weren't many signs to decipher. We'd have asked for directions if we'd seen any-one to ask, but there were no other cars and the few scattered ranch houses we passed were set no less than a half mile back from the main dirt road. They seemed to reek of unassailable privacy, although I knew from past experience that a hapless out-of-stater would likely be treated with amused curiosity and then sent off in the right direction. We crossed and re-crossed some upper forks of the same stream we'd fished the day before, but that wasn't much help, since a detailed map of that drainage looks like a half-eaten plate of spaghetti. Most of these streams wouldn't have been much even in normal flows, but now many were down to trickles.

This was big, open, flat, fabulously empty country ringed by low mountains in the far distance in every direction. Now and then there'd be a dip down to a creek and a solidly built Civilian Conservation Corps bridge dating to the 1930s. Far-ther on there might be a lip of rimrock sheltering a few squat, compact pines and junipers from the prevailing wind, but mostly it was flat sage country littered with boulders that looked like they'd recently dropped from the sky.

We saw jackrabbits and some antelope, but the cattle would still have been in higher, summer range. Except for the road and the barbed-wire fences, the place would have looked pretty much the same a hundred years ago, or a thousand, and parts of it could have passed for the photos of Mars that had recently been sent back by the unmanned rover.

This is one of the rewards of living in the West: the endless drives through apparently endless country, towing a plume of dust behind you, believing you know where you are and where you're going, but knowing, too, that the first stage of being lost is thinking you can't possibly be lost.

The antelope and rabbits in the basin seemed fat enough and the sagebrush looked as grayish-olive and healthy as that scraggly bush ever looks. Sure, it was dusty and the grass was brown, but it's always like that by late summer. Still, last year's snowpack had once again been pitifully low in most places, and the effects of the three-year drought were becoming cumulative.

Naturally, there were local variations. The basin we were driving through didn't look any drier than usual, but it would have to have been drier than it was back home. The drainage here is comparatively low for the West, with most of the mountains only reaching to around 8,000 feet and only one lonesome peak pushing to just over 10,000. On our home water, the mountains go to 14,000 feet and wring more water from the passing fronts, keeping the high country wetter and the streams running higher. The snowpack in our four local drainages had been below average, but still higher than in most others, so we had to travel some distance from home to see the full effects of the drought, and we were humbly grateful for that.

The wildfires started in early June that year: dozens of major blazes around the West that, before they were all out, burned over 620,000 acres in Colorado alone, or about 600,000 acres more than in an average fire season. Those blazes included the Big Elk Fire in the national forest a few miles from my house, which started from the hot catalytic converter on a Jeep stalled in dry grass. In more normal conditions this could have just been a spot fire, but although the driver reported it immediately, the weather was hot enough and the woods dry enough that the fire blew up before a crew could reach it.

One morning I saw the plume of smoke from my back porch and it had grown to the size of a thunderhead by noon. A few days later the high school in town was converted to a fire camp with a headquarters inside and hundreds of firefighters from half a dozen states camped in pup tents in the surrounding fields—some of the crews fresh, others shuffled in from other fires. Press briefings were held, staged for the TV cameras with an American flag and an impressive cloud of smoke in the near background, made to look even closer with the squashed perspective of telephoto lenses. That night we made the national news and my mother called.

We watched the fire with the helpless fascination of potential victims, noting the wind direction every half hour and thinking we should be doing something more than standing around and watching, but of course there was nothing to do. Volunteers are turned away for good reason: Untrained civilians are worse than useless on a fire line and usually do more harm than good, and of course there's the problem of liability.

Along with everyone else in that end of the county, I formulated the necessary evacuation plan—fly rods, books, cats, girlfriend. Not necessarily in that order. We were in no immediate danger, but some people trailered their horses down to the fairgrounds anyway because that's not a job you want to do in a panic at the last minute. We live up a dead-end valley, and the knowledge that there's just that one road out makes you a little skittish.

During the day, the fire would blow up, pushed by hot, dry wind. At night, with cooler temperatures and calmer air, it would lie down and the smoke would sink into the valley. By dawn, it stung the eyes, stank like burning railroad ties and you couldn't see a quarter mile, but as the day warmed and the fire stood up again, the draft reversed itself and the air cleared. It was as if the valley was inhaling deeply, holding its breath all night and exhaling in the morning.

The town filled with young firefighters in those distinctive yellow Nomex fireproof shirts. They seemed shy and distant. They didn't want to be interviewed or fawned over as heroes or even accept a free cup of coffee; they just wanted a pay phone to call home on and some sleep.

All the time the fire burned, I had regular, plotless dreams about huge plumes of smoke on the near horizon. These seemed prophetic because I could wake up, look out the window and see the actual plume of smoke.

In our nervousness, some of us even managed to bury some hatchets. I saw a man with whom I'd been having a minor feud. He'd been evacuated from the little settlement of Big Elk Meadows and was staying in a friend's small apartment in a nearby town with his wife, baby and young Labrador retriever. I asked if there was anything I could do, but all he needed was to bring the dog out to my place so it could run around in the open and let off some steam. I said of course, if only for the sake of the dog.

With nothing more constructive to do, I went fishing. Some of us had found that by two o'clock in the afternoon, the sun would sink behind the dense cloud of smoke to the west, shading the creeks and turning the air an autumnal yellowish-orange color. The impression was of an approaching evening thunderstorm and the occasional drone of passing slurry bombers could even have passed for thunder. This fooled the trout completely. The scattered caddis and mayfly hatches that normally wouldn't start until evening came on hours early and the fish, feeling safe under what they must have taken for cloud cover, rose happily to eat them. I took to going up to one of the nearby creeks every day after lunch. I wondered what kind of man would go fishing during a disaster. Then I wondered what kind wouldn't.

By the time it was over, some 4,400 acres had burned and three firefighters had died in crashes of a slurry bomber and a helicopter. In a typical example of a media culture, I might have seen those aircraft go down if I'd been standing out on the porch looking southwest, but I ended up hearing about them on the evening news and the small screen did its usual fine job of making it all seem less than completely real.

The Big Elk Fire didn't take out Big Elk Meadows as everyone assumed it would, but it was the closest possible call and a damned fine job of firefighting. One man who went back to his house afterward said he could stand on the porch and pee into the still-smoldering ashes of the fire. That's a textbook example of what we'd now call a "guy thing," but when you hear it from a man in his late forties, you can pretty accurately judge the distance.

In the end, only one structure was lost: an abandoned homesteader's cabin that was on the historic register. A friend who lives in New York City said over the phone, "I don't believe you guys can burn up four thousand acres and only lose one cabin." I said, "Hey man, it was a really nice cabin."

By the time the Big Elk Fire was 60 percent contained, the reporters and most of the fire crews had left, heading for the next catastrophe, of which there were plenty that summer. A

115

friend predicted a bumper crop of morel mushrooms in the burn the following spring and a pissing match developed between local residents and the U.S. Forest Service, who wouldn't allow a monument to the fallen pilots to be erected on Forest Service land. The stone finally ended up outside the Pinewood Springs firehouse, where, in fact, more people will see it.

The fire had seemed to burn forever, but then when it was out it all seemed to have happened quickly. By the time the hand-painted "God Bless You Firefighters" signs went up around town, all but the mop-up crews had already left.

Sometime in July, with over a dozen fires still burning around the state, the governor said publicly that vacationers might want to rethink their plans to come to Colorado that summer because it had pretty much dried up, blown away and burned down. Within hours the tourist industry pitched a hissy fit that would last for months. (Apparently truth in advertising wasn't in their charter.) On most of the trout streams and lakes, there were fewer fishermen than I'd seen in over thirty years.

With the sky clear and the sun hot and bright again, we went higher up the drainage, where the air was cooler and the hatches started a little earlier in the day. We caught rainbows, browns, brook trout and some fat little greenback cutthroats, more or less as if nothing had happened. It occurred to me that not having your house burn up in a wildfire is a lot like successfully fishing through a drought, in that life is usually filled with more things that *could have* happened than with things that actually did.

Vince and I located the lake we were looking for with a few good hours of daylight left: the hours of late afternoon and evening when trout usually bite best. Once we were close, there were specific landmarks: a German-sounding name on a white mailbox, a cattle guard freshly painted green, then a dirt track along the north side of a fence line. (Good directions are one of the joys of a fisherman's life.) The lake was a fat horseshoe shape, as promised, and it was nicely hidden from view from the dirt road by a slight rise, so you wouldn't know it was there unless you already knew it was there.

The lake had apparently shrunk from around sixty acres to more like forty-five and it had a pretty extensive mud flat around it with the old tracks of raccoons, coyotes and wading birds sunbaked into it. But there it was, still at least a thousand yards across at its widest with some good-sized trout rising on its smooth surface. Some of those trout looked like they'd be just within casting range.

The lake was nestled at the edge of the basin against some low forested foothills. The inlet had slowed to a trickle, but there was enough water left to sustain a narrow grove of pine and aspen that ran along the creek channel like a finger pointing at those rising trout. To the south the sagebrush high plains stretched to the first low hill, blue-green with a hint of dull bronze from the late-afternoon light.

We didn't forget that we'd come to fish, but we did take a few moments to stretch and admire the scene. This is a region that's prone to heat, cold, drought, floods, blizzards, avalanches, hurricane-force chinook winds, skin cancer (from the altitude), rattlesnake bites, tick fever, wildfires, overdevelopment in some areas, rural poverty in others and of course the normal amount of human idiocy in all its forms—but that doesn't mean it isn't paradise.

Chapter 12

I T WAS past dark when we left the little outpost gas station and general store in east-central Wyoming. This place sits at the intersection where highway 487 joins 220, the road that parallels the North Platte River below Gray Reef Dam. It's the last chance for gas and coffee before you head off on the back way down to Colorado, so you hope it's open. If it's not, it's a forty-mile round-trip to the next nearest gas on the east end of Casper, and if you head south across Shirley Basin with less than half a tank, you might not make it.

Chris got out ahead of us, towing his drift boat, anxious to spend a day with Betsy before coming back up to guide more late-season fishermen on the river. Like many fishing guides, the guy's seasonal life is a blur of long hours on the water, long drives, road food, poor accommodations and quick stops at home. He seems to love it (you'd have to) but I think by fall it becomes a little bit of a grind.

Vince and I dawdled a little, talking to a guy about snag-

118

ging paddlefish on the Missouri River in Montana while we microwaved our burgers and tried to determine the age of the coffee. It looked pretty lethal, so I was adding some hot water to take the edge off. Vince wondered why I'd consider drinking the stuff at all. He tends to drink Coke on the road, which is safer in that it doesn't deteriorate in a matter of hours, but to an addict, good coffee may be better than bad coffee, but bad coffee is still better than none.

Out on the highway, Vince had just gotten the big Ford pickup to cruising speed and I'd just taken the first tentative sip of my hot coffee when I glanced out the windshield and yelled, "Deer!"

They were standing in the middle of the road gazing blankly into our high beams. Vince remembers three or four, I remember six. However many there were, Vince stood on the brakes hard, just short of putting us into a skid, and steered between them expertly, as if he did this sort of thing every day. He couldn't have missed any of them by much, but he missed them all.

Vince's "Big Gulp" of Coke was all over the floor in a sticky puddle and I was wet with hot coffee from my eyeballs to my knees. It seemed funny as hell, and we pulled over to the side of the road and sat there laughing like maniacs. A pickup coming along behind us slowed briefly to see if we needed help, then sped up again, apparently figuring we were either okay or too crazy to deal with.

We'd floated two good stretches of the North Platte River in the last two days and now we were anxious to get the five-hour drive back home over with, hoping to get in around midnight or one o'clock. Not that it really mattered. It's just that an American behind the wheel sets himself a goal and a time limit, if only to avoid standing by the side of a dark road howling at the moon. That's why we were driving too fast at night down a highway that's notorious for collisions between deer and automobiles. I've never driven this thing in daylight without seeing at least half a dozen deer carcasses on the shoulders, not to mention the occasional antelope, plus cottontails, jackrabbits, raccoons, skunks and the odd coyote or rattlesnake. Even in a part of the world where more game is killed by cars than by hunters, the carnage is impressive.

I like to think that fishermen eventually absorb the pace set by flowing water and end up going through life in a more or less relaxed way: so much so that at times the rest of the world might think we're a little dim-witted. Maybe that's true (I hope so), but then it always amazes me that as soon as we climb behind a steering wheel at the end of the day, we're right back to going balls to the wall.

The conditions on the river had been what you'd call about right for the season. The water was a little low, making for some skinny spots for the drift boat, but then the likely places for fish to be were smaller and easier to read, and in the spots where you could get out of the boat, the wading was more forgiving.

Of course a river *should* be lower in the fall, but this one in this stretch is a controlled tailwater that's immune to natural flows to some degree, but not to the vagaries of water calls. Rivers like this actually mimic what they used to do before the dams, but the changes are often magnified and sudden.

If you check stream-flow charts on a computer, you'll see that the graph showing ten days' worth of flows on an undammed stream makes the kind of sinuous line you'd expect from any measurement of natural water: up on hot days when more snowpack melts, lower on cool days, with smaller bumps and hollows for day and night. The graph for rivers like the North Platte is more likely to be made up of straight vertical and horizontal lines that look like a stairway designed by an architect on LSD.

Both days on the river were windy—this is Wyoming, after all—but it wasn't too cold and there were banks of high clouds that kept the sun off the water at least half the time. When the sun did slip in under the clouds late in the day, it lit up the rolling high plains in the warm grays, browns, tans and olives you'd see in a Russell Chatham landscape or, for that matter, on the clothing of upscale fly fishers and ornamental ranchers.

There'd been very few other boats on the water, but we'd passed two guys in a dory who spotted us as out-of-staters in the same mysterious, nonverbal way we identified them as locals. They gave us the hairy eyeball for being on their river, but I'd been glared at by three-hundred-pound cops in the South in the 1960s, so I didn't think anything of it.

Chris was off duty, out with friends instead of guiding, so we switched off on the oars and he got to fish. (Once we passed another drift boat and the guide yelled, "Hey, Chris, you're in the wrong seat.") If I spent as much time as Chris does on the river helping other people fish, but not fishing myself, I think I'd be frantic when I finally got a rod in my hand. But he always seems relaxed and polished.

A lot of the most experienced guides I know have that capacity. It's not that they're detached—although that's how it can look—it's just that they seem to fish more out of inquisitiveness than the rest of us. They wonder if there's a fish in that hard-to-reach spot over there; the one where the clients never cast. They wonder not so much which flies work, but which flies work best, and at what depth with what kind of retrieve. Hand a good guide a fly rod on familiar water and he'll invariably start to experiment because he already knows how to catch the fish.

I kept an eye on Chris as well as I could while I was casting myself or rowing the boat. I mean, here's a good fisherman who knows this river inside out, and you can learn more by watching someone like that for an hour than you can by fishing for days on your own. Guides are better than most (including writers) at explaining how things are done, but many of the best fishermen do subtle things that they're not completely conscious of. There's the nervous little mends that keep the line lying just right on the water, the retrieve that looks like a steady pull until you notice a little kick at the end, or maybe just unblinking concentration. This is what the old-timers meant when they said, "You're not holding your mouth right."

A lot of people nymph-fish the North Platte in the fall and they do well, but we like to fish it with streamers. They're no more efficient, just more fun, with lots of long throws, hard strikes and the casting gymnastics you have to go through to make sure your streamer is always swimming against the current. And of course there are those days in the colder water of spring and fall when streamers bring up the bigger, more aggressive trout.

Just a few days earlier, Chris had been out with a client who rolled a huge brown trout. The fish flashed a streamer twice without eating and they both got a good look at it. Chris guessed that it weighed well over ten pounds and was no less than thirty inches long, in a class with some of the sea-run browns he used to guide for in Argentina. When he told us about it, he got more excited than he usually gets about a fish, which told us more about the thing than the description.

We were all casting similar rigs: long eight-weight rods, sink-tip lines and short leaders. The trick on this trip, as with most streamer fishing, was getting the streamer down to the depth where the fish were holding, which in the cool fall water tends to be pretty deep. They might chase it back up, sometimes almost to the surface—where they'd invariably see the boat and spook at the last instant—but it was only after you put your fly almost on the bottom that you could start worrying about which pattern to use and how to retrieve it.

We all caught plenty of fish, but the times when Chris and I were both casting, he seemed to get about half again more than I did. That's mostly because he's that much better than I am (and I've gotten used to it) but it may also have had something to do with his line.

He was fishing one of those new systems with the interchangeable tips, and he had on a long, skinny sink-tip that cut the wind better and sank quicker than my conventional high-density sink-tip. That means he'd be retrieving his streamer while I was still throwing upstream mends trying to get my line to sink deep enough. It was impressive, and I decided on the spot to run right out and buy one of those things when I got home.

The main difference between me and Chris, aside from age, is that he's as up on all the newest tackle as I am devoted to (or stuck with) the old stuff, although it's interesting how little difference that usually makes. When it comes down to just fishing, it hardly seems to matter whether you're using this year's model graphite rod with the hottest new line or a forty-year-old bamboo with the one line still on the market that hasn't changed since the 1960s. Nine times out of ten, new gear isn't the solution to a fishing problem, but then every once in a while it is, and there's no use denying it. It's in this gradual way that I'm being dragged kicking and screaming into the modern world.

As it turned out, the fishing was best in the mornings and evenings and better under clouds than bright sun, pretty much as you'd expect, since fishing clichés are usually accurate. There were a few times when the fish wanted white streamers and a few other times when they seemed to like black and purple or a Muddler Minnow with a yellow marabou underwing, but mostly it was yellow or yellow mixed with brown, as on the old Platte River Special from the 1950s.

Chris's latest version of the Platte River worked well. It has the same mixed brown and yellow marabou Spey-style hackle as his last incarnation of the pattern, but the wings have grown longer and it has sprouted a thin strip of red goose for flash. (Chris's flies are prettier and more elegant than most guide patterns, but they still have that deceptive simplicity.) He's been adjusting this fly for quite a while now and I wonder if it'll ever settle down into an established pattern or if he'll just keep fiddling with it to keep a step ahead of the fish.

Of course guides have a tremendous advantage when it comes to trying out new patterns. They can give them to their clients and end up showing them to more trout in a few months than most of us could in five years. This tends to accelerate their evolution.

We all landed several rainbows twenty inches and better and plenty of smaller ones. Even the fifteen-inchers fought well enough to take some line off the reel, and Vince and I thought it was just fine. So did Chris, although he added that it wasn't the best two days of fishing he'd ever seen there. But then he's seen more days than most and that enormous brown trout could raise your expectations a notch or two.

Still, it's a real pleasure not to have to say, "Yeah, it's good now, but you should have seen it in the old days." The river is in fine shape, the shortage of water notwithstanding. There are still ten-pound trout in there, and the fact that you'll probably never hook one—let alone land it—doesn't mean a thing except that you'll be back with your newfangled fly line and your best copies of the latest streamer patterns Chris has been fooling around with. There's always something that keeps you coming back.

On the drive home that night, Vince slowed down some after the hair-raising near miss with the deer, and driving close to the speed limit added half an hour to the trip across Shirley Basin. You can remind yourself that not all that long ago you'd have had to do this on horseback and it would have taken days, but it still doesn't keep you from getting impatient.

I'd spilled my coffee, but the adrenaline rush of the near wreck kept me awake and alert. We made a game of spotting deer and jackrabbits on the side of the road all the way to Laramie, where I got a fresh cup at a Kum & Go from a device that looked like it came off the bridge of the *Enterprise*. The coffee was real good, but the lights were too bright and there was a disturbing electronic hum in the place that was impossible to locate. Listening to that through shift after shift at minimum wage would explain the clerk's crazy eyes.

Vince was talking on his cell phone out in the parking lot. He had a finger in one ear because of the boom box in an idling hot rod. I remembered that the day before on the river Chris had climbed a low hill to make a call. Apparently it's now part of the lore of this river that the crest of this particular ridge is the one place where you can get a signal. That no longer shocks me (I long ago added it to the growing list of things you never used to see) but I do always wonder who you need to talk to while you're fishing.

In the gas station bathroom, I noticed that yet another rubber machine had been turned into a "Family Planning Center" to reflect the new sensitivity, but they were still selling "Super Studded" condoms as if they were snow tires. I had to remind myself that this is indeed the same world in which trout fishing takes place; it's just a different part of it.

Chapter 13

I T RAINED more or less steadily for five days. It was mostly somewhere between a drizzle and a sprinkle, the kind of thing you could stay out in almost tolerably with the right gear, but which would sooner or later penetrate just a bit too close for comfort. Sometimes it came down hard enough to make you want to go hide for a while, and even when the rain tapered off momentarily, the trees continued to drip.

Sometimes what fell looked like snow in the air and rain on the ground in the same way that physicists say light sometimes behaves like particles and other times like waves. I've heard this called "snoosh" for lack of a better word in English. It never rained quite hard enough to muddy the river or put the fish down. Still, it rained, and that became a central fact. Sometimes you'd see a local drought-stricken fisherman gazing up at it with the blank but wondrous expression of a child on a first white Christmas. Of course it had rained some during the drought—just nowhere near enough—but this was the kind of profound soaker we'd almost forgotten.

Daytime temperatures were only in the low 40s, but at night the thick cloud cover held in what little warmth there was, so it stayed just above freezing. It was the ideal ambient temperature in which to age a side of beef. We wouldn't have minded if the nights had been colder because you can crack off ice and shake off snow, but rain soaks in and stays with you. Some mornings there was a skiff of snow dusting the ridges above camp, but down along the river it was just a gloriously soggy meat locker.

Mike Clark and A.K. had already been there for a day by the time Ed and I arrived in separate vehicles from separate parts of the state, and they had the camp set up nicely. A.K.'s old kitchen box and wobbly folding table were under a rain fly stretched between two trees and propped up with an elaborate series of poles and tie-downs that someone would eventually trip over. It wasn't a huge tarp, but it made a dry space big enough for four fishermen to get in out of the rain—provided they were smart enough to do that.

It did slow to a drizzle just long enough for Ed and me to quickly get our tents set up, and that was a break. I've never been able to put a camp together in an outright rain without getting everything good and wet, including the sleeping bag, pad and the tent itself—both inside and out. And of course in that kind of weather, whatever gets wet will stay that way for the duration.

There were times when it would have been handy to build a fire to warm up and dry out a little, but we couldn't do that. After a third dry summer and the dozens of wildfires around the state, which got Colorado on the national news more than once as a disaster area, an open-fire ban had been in effect for months. The governor had finally lifted the ban a few weeks before as some much-needed rain and early-autumn snows began to fall, but some places, including the county we were camped in, had decided to leave it on. The woods were dripping wet, but the people behind the desks were spooked and didn't want to make a dumb mistake late in the season. I can't say I blamed them.

But rain is what we'd been hoping for, not only generally but specifically, because this was one of those rivers that fish best in foul weather. We'd gone for the mayfly hatches and mayflies have a perverse love of chilly days, cloudy skies and at least light rain. So do trout, especially the big ones. The theory is that they feel more confident about feeding up at the surface under the relative cover of a cold, dark, drizzly day, but I'm not sure it isn't just cussedness. You're not supposed to anthropomorphize, but if fish hated fishermen you couldn't really blame them. Fishing and camping in these conditions are among the things that make fishermen seem crazy to the great mass of unimaginative people, but then few fishermen care what they think.

After breakfast most mornings—say around nine o'clock or so—there'd be a sparse hatch of size 18 or 20 Blue-Winged Olives and a few trout would begin to rise. You could get some on a dry fly, which is how A.K. fished it, but I usually did better with an unweighted nymph squeezed wet and fished an inch or so under the surface.

A.K. and I have been arguing for over twenty years about which method is better. The dry fly is prettier and often more unlikely, especially early in a thin hatch when there are a lot more nymphs under water than there are duns on the surface. Drifting a fly under water is a little more efficient, but then detecting the take to a tiny, invisible nymph with no strike in-

129

dicator is a lot harder, so you usually don't catch any more fish. Neither of us really cares all that much about which way is better; it's just something to talk about.

The real hatch would begin around two in the afternoon and last for at least a few hours. It would be all Blue-Winged Olives for a while, then Olives mixed with Pale Morning Duns, then those two mixed with a few bigger Sulphurs. Scattered in there at various times you could also see small Red Quills, the odd Flavilinea, maybe some caddis flies, or even a few rare, late-season Green Drakes, any of which a trout could decide to eat to the exclusion of everything else. The hatches would come in slow, multiple, overlapping waves, building to lots of steady rises, then slipping back to a few scattered, occasional rings, then gradually pulsing back just when you thought it was over.

There'd be a wallowing dorsal fin in a moderate current as a trout took nymphs just under the surface. In faster water you'd see those quick rolls as fish took either floating emergers or duns. A splashy rise could mean a fast-swimming caddis pupa or just an excited fish. The light was gray and flat, making it hard to see into the water, but now and then you'd catch the dull flash of a suspended trout eating nymphs a foot or two under the surface. Down in the slower tails of the runs, a fish would wallow, then sip, then bulge, then show his head back to the gill covers, eating whatever came by.

The easier trout would stay in a single spot where you could put one fly after another over him until you hit the right drift and pattern or he either spooked or finally revealed himself as uncatchable. The harder ones would slide around, working upstream, then fading down, then scooting to the side. Wherever you put your fly, the fish would be a foot away, facing the other direction.

You could try to match your pattern to what a particular fish seemed to be eating or, in a different mood, just tie on a fly you liked and go looking for a trout that fancied it as much as you did, but you'd always keep an eye out for the size-14 Sulphurs. On this river at this time of year, the trout have a real sweet tooth for those medium-sized, yellowish mayflies. Their hatches are sporadic and never thick, but when even a scattering of Sulphurs is on the water, the trout almost always prefer them to anything else. A pulse of them might only last a few minutes—just long enough to change flies and get in a few casts—but when it happened it could be a reprieve from the usual difficulties.

Whatever fly you'd choose, the drift had to be good: no splash, no drag and right to the fish. Trout on rich rivers with heavy hatches get to be picky eaters; add the kind of fishing pressure this one sometimes sees, and they get paranoid on top of that. It was a nice struggle. Lots of trout were caught, but there were lots more that weren't, so you could never quite manage to get cocky.

One afternoon I spent a long time on a big brown. At least I think it was a brown. Squinting through rain and gray light, I thought I saw the butter-colored sides, but it may have just been wishful thinking. He was rising on the far side of the main current in a little notch in the bank: the kind of divot that would be left when a rock the size of a washtub finally let go and plopped into the river. He was behind a screen of overhanging willow limbs low enough so that, wading thigh-deep, you had to crouch a little to see his head break the surface. It looked like a head that would be attached to a trout no less then twenty inches long, but it would be there and gone so quickly that, again, I couldn't be sure.

I struggled with the cast. It had to be sidearm, slightly downstream and across with a little air mend that looped the leader upstream, but still let the fly miss the overhanging limb by an inch or two. It took me several tries to snake one in there, and when I did, I slapped the water too hard with the fly and put the fish down. I tensed and crouched as if just the right body English could rewind the event and make it right, but the mistake was already history.

I waded downstream and cast the same Blue-Winged Olive parachute to a smaller trout rising amid the raindrops in open water. After a dozen or so tries, I caught him. When I looked back upstream, I could see quiet rings coming out from under the willow, which meant my fish was rising again.

I waded back into position, made the cast well enough, and although the drift was six inches off, the fish turned and took the fly anyway. I set too fast and pulled the hook out of his mouth before he even had it. He was big, he was my fish. I flubbed it.

Twenty minutes later when the fish started feeding again, I hooked the bush right above his head, tried to gently tug the fly loose and spooked him with a shower of willow leaves. Then I yanked harder and broke off the fly.

It took the fish forever to start rising again, but this time I made the right cast and drift with a Pale Morning Dun. He calmly ate the fly. I calmly hesitated for half a heartbeat and set the hook. It was beautiful. There was a loud splash and I could feel the little hook just tick his lip as it came loose.

This is when you remind yourself that no fish anywhere owes you a damned thing, but it was still a trout I'd dream about. In the dream he'd be much, much bigger and he'd somehow be more than just a trout, so his loss would be final and tragic. This could be one where I'd wake up sweating to wander the house at three in the morning, bumping into walls and stepping on cats. (I do dream about fish regularly. Also sex and firewood. I don't get it either.)

I'd spent almost two hours on the same trout, most of it waiting for him to start rising again after I'd put him down and watching rain drip from the hood of my raincoat. I'd screwed it up four times and the last time was permanent. A trout that feels the hook is gone for good. And this was a big, dumb fish that was willing to be caught by a fisherman who was up to it. I wondered if I was losing my touch. I wondered if I ever really *had* the touch. But then you have to get over that kind of thing quickly. I mean, if temporarily losing your chops meant the game was up, I'd have been done for long ago.

I gave up (the moment does come when you simply give up), waded down to the next pool and promptly hooked and landed a big, fat twenty-inch brown in bright fall colors. The fish hadn't been rising, but it was an easy first cast to an obvious spot where I thought one might be. He ran for a snag, but I turned him, wore him down in the tail of the pool and netted him on the first try.

So is this like childhood, where every little tragedy is somehow pulled out in the end? You know, lose your balloon, get an ice-cream cone to show that fairness prevails? This late in the game, I can't be sure if I'm recalling my actual childhood, or subconsciously rerunning old episodes of *Leave It to Beaver.*

It was going on supper time. I was badly chilled from standing in cold water in the rain all afternoon. I walked back to camp—having decided to quit while ahead—and found A.K. under the shelter of the tarp making a fresh pot of coffee and looking ripe for a long story. Perfect.

• • •

That night we sat around my little propane lantern under the rain fly and talked, as four old fishing friends will do. It was the latest installment in a conversation that's been going on since about 1975, but beyond that I couldn't tell you much of what was said. I'm sure we all got into what we were working on because there's always something. Somewhere among us there are always books, articles and columns being written, videotapes being produced, classes being taught and, in Mike's case, the latest in a body of handmade bamboo fly rods dating back over twenty years. It never surprises me to see these guys do well because I know them as the kind of people who would. On the other hand, I also remember us all as much younger goofballs trying to figure out how to fish properly while still making some kind of a living, and it still amazes me that, to one extent or another, we've all managed it.

And then someone did mention that a fire would feel good. Someone else said it was too damned wet to get a fire going. Someone else said it was raining too hard to stand out next to a fire anyway. That's all I remember.

We took turns warming our hands around the propane lantern's single mantle, then retired to our pickups where we sat with the heaters running to get warm before crawling into the sleeping bags. Under the dome light I'd do a little reading in Mark Spragg's great memoir, *Where Rivers Change Direction.* It was mostly about his early hardships, all of which were worse than having to get a little wet in order to catch some trout.

Mike and Ed pulled out the next day, loosely packing their soggy gear because it would all have to be hauled out and dried later anyway. A.K. and I hung around camp for a while and then did some slow-paced fishing—the kind you can get into after several days and many fish. I didn't go back to the trout under the bush because that whole episode seemed perfectly self-contained as it was. I'd told A.K. where the fish was, but he didn't try for it either.

The last evening in camp, the sky cleared and we saw stars and a nearly full waxing moon before we turned in. With the lid of clouds off, we imagined we could feel a breeze coming straight up from the ground as the last of the meager warmth rose into the sky. We decided to leave in the morning after drying out our gear during a leisurely breakfast. It was going to be a brutally cold night, but tomorrow would be a lovely, warm, sunny day and the fishing would suck.

I was comfortable enough in my sleeping bag that night, but it was deathly cold inside the tent and the moonlight made a green, liquid glow through the nylon walls. I woke up once during the night with the distinct impression that I was submerged in cold water, but wasn't drowning. I wondered what the hell that could mean, and went back to sleep.

Chapter 14

MIKE PRICE and I made two trips down to the South Platte River the December after the fires. Both days were the kind we sometimes get here in the winter, in a state that sees an average of over three hundred sunny days every year. The weather was blue and bright and for a few hours in the middle of the day it was comfortable enough as long as you dressed for it and stayed in the sun. But then down in the canyon the shadows swallow you early and the air chills so that even a little breeze can slice right to the skin through layers of fleece, wool and down. Once that starts to happen, your wet fly line freezes in the guides after three or four casts and has to be chipped out by hand, so the standard twenty good drifts with a nymph through a likely-looking run can result in some drudgery. By three thirty or four o'clock, you tell yourself that you are in fact tough enough to stick it out, but if you can't fish, what's the point?

December is traditionally the slowest month on this river,

but good fishing isn't unheard of. Sometimes fish graze actively on midge pupae and sometimes there's a Blue-Winged Olive hatch that's either the last of the fall hatch or the beginnings of the seldom-seen winter hatch. So it *is* worth going, aside from just getting out of the house. But that year we mostly just wanted to see how the river had weathered the Hayman Fire.

Of the dozens of serious fires around the state the previous summer, this thing had been the real monster. It was started accidentally by a Forest Service employee who claimed that things got out of hand while she was angrily burning a love letter from her ex-husband. It eventually burned 137,000 acres and became the biggest single wildfire in Colorado's recorded history.

The blaze had scorched the earth right to the water line at Cheesman Reservoir, but except for a few small spot fires started by flying embers, it missed the river below. The official Forest Service incident map showed an amoeboid burn area with two stubby horns hooking roughly northeast around the river. A firefighter friend had predicted that back when the woods were still burning. A fire of that size makes its own weather, he said, so it will burn out the ridges unstoppably, but it won't burn downhill against its own updraft.

At its height, that fire was totally out of control and burning directly toward the western suburbs of Denver. Naturally news crews from around the country and in some cases the world smelled an epic disaster and gathered like vultures around a half-dead cow. They all but ignored the daily loss of mountain homes and cabins as they waited for what they thought would be the main event. It was not what you'd call a dignified performance.

That was in late June. Five months later, surrounded by the

same green ponderosa pines, the South Platte seemed weirdly untouched by the fire. The only obvious effect on the river was that the bottom was stained black from soot and ash, more around Deckers, a little less upstream in Cheesman Canyon, where the water is steeper and faster. According to the Division of Wildlife biologists I talked to, some trout farther downriver were killed after the fire, not from being smothered by ash as you might expect, but because the late-summer sun shining on that dark bottom in low August stream flows raised the water temperature too high.

A lot of the river's aquatic vegetation had died from the soot, but even by December there was fresh new growth using the dead weeds and the nutrients from the ash as fertilizer. There were worries about the insect populations, but by September fishermen were reporting at least passable Blue-Winged Olive mayfly hatches and some fish were being caught.

Still, the trout were hit hard in places. Division of Wildlife biologist Barry Nehring (known to local fly fishers as "Mr. South Platte") said that a survey done after the fire showed fewer trout in the river between Deckers and Scraggy View than he'd seen in the last twenty years, and he was worried about a catastrophic event the following spring. The roots that kept a tenuous hold on the loose soil had been incinerated and Nehring said he'd seen post-fire flash floods where a thunderstorm dumping two inches of rain had sent a slug of silt "the consistency of wet cement" down a river, causing trout to literally swim out on the banks trying to escape it.

So, that winter biologists and fishermen were left hoping for a late winter and spring wet enough to break the three-year drought and flush the soot from the streambed, but not wet enough to choke the river with mud. That was a big order, but then the South Platte's history, like that of too many other rivers in America, has been one of catastrophes barely avoided or at least survived, so there was reason to hope.

Once upon a time, way back in the mid 1800s, the South Platte was a pristine trout stream filled with native greenback cutthroats. The earliest fishing would have been done by the prospectors and settlers who arrived shortly after William Green Russell discovered gold in the drainage in 1858, and a good deal of that was market fishing done with nets and dynamite. In 1861, the *Rocky Mountain News* in Denver reported matter-of-factly on a "wagon load of fish" that came out of the South Platte to be sold at the market on Blake Street. Fisheries biologists now say that even under ideal conditions, greenbacks rarely grow longer than about thirteen inches. One can only imagine how many trout of that size it would take to fill a wagon.

By 1870 there was a territorial law prohibiting "the use of explosives for fishing" (an early example of tackle restrictions) and market fishing was outlawed completely in 1876 when Colorado became a state, but enforcement was thin at best and courts often winked at offenders. This was the frontier, after all, where men were men and trout were a cheap delicacy.

It was also in the 1870s that the Denver, South Park & Pacific Railroad pushed a line through the South Platte Canyon, allowing easier access for fishermen. The trains were so popular with anglers that in 1893 the railroad—by then the Colorado & Southern—began running trains called Fisherman's Specials up the canyon on weekends. The fishing trains continued to run until the 1930s, when the first passable road was built.

The heavy sport- and market-fishing pressure must have cleaned out the native greenback cutthroats pretty quickly. According to angling historian John Monnett, they were gone by the 1880s. Nehring thinks they held out for a few more decades, until the early 1900s, but the exact date hardly matters now. Either way, there hasn't been a native trout in the river for a hundred years.

The first records of state-stocked rainbow trout date to 1882, and in 1895, the Colorado & Southern began stocking 250,000 rainbows annually in the South Platte to replace the vanishing cutthroats and help keep the fishing trains lucrative.

Brown trout were first stocked by the state in the 1890s, barely a decade after they were first introduced into North America from Europe, and browns continued to be stocked off and on, officially and otherwise, until the 1940s. In the early 1920s the exclusive Wigwam Club above Deckers was also stocking browns from its own private hatchery. Other fish introduced into the Platte before 1901 included brook trout, steelhead, grayling, American shad, walleyes and northern pike, none of which took.

The Wigwam Club is still there and it still isn't much liked by many nonmembers, but by now it's just that stretch of private water that separates the lower roadside river from the wilder, though often more crowded canyon above. Things were different early on, though. There was a lot of trespassing, vandalism and even reports of arson. Fishermen naturally didn't like the idea of a bunch of rich guys closing off part of their river, while a privately published history of the club suggests that at least some of those rich guys considered it their responsibility to close as much of the river as possible to the common rabble.

But it's the rare fisherman who drools over the club's private water anymore. There are effectively wild people's trout living in the public water upstream and down, while the club raises its own big ones and then dumps them into the river. As high-toned as it might seem, fishing there now would have to be like drowning cheese balls at a fish farm. Over the years I've gotten two invitations to fish the Wigwam Club water, but when I didn't exhibit the expected degree of fawning gratitude, both invitations were rescinded.

In the late 1800s, there were protests over the proposed Cheesman Dam on the South Platte. Colorado was still sparsely populated and Denver wasn't much of a city, but even back then there were people to whom water meant nothing but money, and seeing it just run in a river was like watching gold dust being flushed down a toilet.

An 1899 editorial in the *Denver Times* said the dam would "ruin the river for trout fishing," but as it turned out it didn't. The bottom-draw dam was completed in 1905 and it created what we now know as the classic tailwater effect: more uniform water temperatures, enriched water chemistry, incredible numbers of small aquatic insects, lots of big, fat trout and a nearly year-round growing season for the fish. Given the economics of water, that probably happened by accident—or at least as an afterthought—but it happened.

By the early 1900s, the South Platte was what we'd now call a premier trout stream, that is, full of big trout, highly publicized and crowded, at least by the standards of the time. It was also a heavily stocked fishery. In April 1911, *Denver Municipal Facts,* a weekly magazine published by the city of Denver, reported that between 1904 and 1909 a total of "15 million young trout" had been stocked in the South Platte. That issue included grainy photos of men in suits and derbies and women in long skirts and parasols fishing the Platte with fifteen-foot fly rods. I desperately want to think it was a staged photo op.

The record trout from the South Platte in 1911, six years

after Cheesman Dam was completed, supposedly weighed sixteen pounds, although up through the 1930s reports of big trout from the river usually hovered between six and eight pounds. Even allowing for the usual exaggeration, the fishing was good, and it stayed good for the better part of a century, with periodic stocking and probably some natural reproduction.

The South Platte became famous for its heavy mayfly and midge hatches, and as a river where you fished for large trout with small flies. It was said that you could fish an entire season and never tie on a fly bigger than a size 16. By the 1970s, that was revised to a size 18 and they were beginning to call that kind of fishing "technical."

There was also a tradition of bamboo-rod building that grew up around the South Platte. Goodwin Granger made rods in Denver between 1918 and 1931. Granger died in 1931, but the Wright & McGill Company continued to make bamboo rods under the Granger name, using the original tapers, until the early 1960s. Bill Phillipson, who was known to fish the South Platte often and well, originally worked for Granger, then Wright & McGill and then went off to form the Phillipson Rod Company after World War II. Charlie Jenkins, who also fishes the South Platte, began making bamboo rods around 1960. The Jenkins Rod Company, which now includes Charlie's son Steve, is still in business.

All those makers naturally wanted to sell fly rods to any fishermen anywhere, but they all became known for rods of medium length and weight that cast well at short to moderate ranges and were delicate enough to fish small flies and light leaders, but that still had the backbone to play large trout. That's a lot to ask from a fly rod, but it's exactly what you need for the South Platte.

Being a sentimental type, I have a couple of old Wright &

McGill Grangers and an 8 1/2-foot Phillipson that I like to fish on the Platte, partly out of nostalgia, but also because their actions are perfectly suited to the water.

I also remember running into Charlie Jenkins on the river sometime in the 1980s. He was fishing a favorite pool of his just downstream from Deckers and I just happened to be fishing one of his rods, a two-piece, eight-foot five-weight that I'd recently bought used. I was happy to see him. He was happy to see his old rod being fished and shyly asked me how I liked it. (Charlie is the only rod maker I've ever met with a normal-sized ego.) I told him I liked it a lot, and not just to be polite. It was a sweet moment.

The style of nymph fishing in which a small nymph is tied on eighteen or twenty inches below a split shot and fished on a short line is often called the South Platte method and stories about it on the river date back at least to the 1930s, when a member of the Wigwam Club was asked to stop fishing that way or be ejected from the club for catching too many trout. To be fair, though, the method is so obvious and so much like bait fishing that it was probably independently invented at one time or another on every river in America, although it wasn't until the 1970s that it began to be seen as anything more than cheating.

The South Platte is touted as a wild-trout fishery, but it wasn't until the 1970s that the Division of Wildlife began to manage the river for self-sustaining trout populations. Gold Medal and Wild Trout waters were established with tackle restrictions and reduced bag and size limits, and in 1976 the Cheesman Canyon stretch became Colorado's first catch-and-release area. Most fishermen seemed to like the new rules. The division said that the most restrictive regulations drew the biggest crowds. They took that as a good thing.

Some supplemental stocking of catchable-sized rainbows continued in the river below Cheesman Canyon until 1983, but the trend at the time was toward wild-trout management, so stocking between Deckers and Scraggy View ceased for the next fourteen years. The highest population of trout ever recorded in that stretch was between 1986 and 1988, and many of us fondly remember that Golden Age when big trout were stacked in the pools like cordwood. To this day, I've never seen that many trout in so small a space outside of a hatchery.

The trout upstream in Cheesman Canyon were another story. The canyon is a rugged three miles of river that was by-passed by tracks and roads and is still only accessible on foot. According to Barry Nehring, the canyon hasn't been stocked since 1952, when some rainbows were planted. At that time it was predominantly a brown-trout fishery, probably populated by escapees from the Wigwam Club over the previous few decades. A creel census done between 1952 and 1954 showed that fishermen were catching almost nothing but browns, and things stayed that way more or less into the mid 1970s.

But then in the springs of 1977 and 1978, conditions for rainbow spawning were the best they'd ever been in the canyon and things began to turn around. A survey done by the division in 1979 showed the canyon to be 70 to 80 per-cent rainbows. These would have been wild fish: the descen-dants of those rainbows stocked almost thirty years earlier as well as a few others that had worked their way up from downstream.

By the 1980s, the South Platte, and Cheesman Canyon in particular, had developed a national reputation for large wild trout and very difficult fishing and the river was getting lots of coverage in the fishing press. Sometime in the early 1980s, I submitted a story about Cheesman Canyon to a national fishing magazine and the editor wrote back saying he already had a dozen identical stories on hand and adding, "Christ, don't you Colorado guys fish anywhere else?" As you'd expect, the river began to draw tremendous crowds. It was the kind of popular acceptance that encouraged the Division of Wildlife to establish other catch-and-release areas around the state.

Water officials had been eyeing the potential dam site at the confluence of the South Platte and its North Fork (some twenty miles below Cheesman) since the 1890s, but Two Forks Dam was first seriously proposed in the 1960s. Then in 1986 the Denver Water Board filed for a permit to build the dam. The resulting reservoir would have flooded the river from the confluence upstream to the town of Deckers, inundating many homes and turning some of the best water on the river into a steep-sided lake.

The controversy over the proposal was enormous—much more so than the token resistance to Cheesman over eighty years earlier. There were demonstrations, public meetings and lots of press coverage, including reams of angry letters to editors. "Stop Two Forks" T-shirts became a fashion statement on the South Platte and signs saying "All this will be under water" sprouted along the river downstream from Deckers.

Before it was all over, proponents of the project spent $40 million pursuing federal Environmental Protection Agency approval of the dam. Opponents spent considerably less, but won anyway. In March 1989, the Army Corps of Engineers approved the permit to build Two Forks Dam, but the following year, William Reilly, then head of the EPA, vetoed the permit, citing "unacceptable adverse effects," including "loss and damage to fisheries."

Many of us who had gone to the river to say goodbye went back to say hello again, beginning a tradition of trips where you went to fish, and did, but also just to pay a visit to the poor beleaguered old river to see how she was doing. Things went along more or less smoothly for a few years, and the only complaints about the South Platte were about the ubiquitous crowds of fishermen. But then whirling disease appeared.

Whirling disease is caused by a microscopic parasite with an unpronounceable Latin name and a complicated life cycle that can be carried by larger trout without any ill effects, but that kills many small ones. The symptoms are blackened tails, skeletal deformities and tail chasing, hence the name.

The parasites arrived in the U.S. in the 1950s, carried from Europe in imported fish. The disease spread to hatcheries and then to rivers through the stocking of infected fish. It was first noticed in Colorado in the 1980s and it spread quickly, again largely through stocking. The parasite was identified in the South Platte near Deckers in 1990.

To a fisherman, the effects of whirling disease seem sudden and drastic. Larger fish carry the parasite, but are unaffected, so as the young trout die out, all you ever catch are the big ones. The river seems fine—better than it's ever been, in fact—until those older fish die off and the river seems to have been emptied of trout overnight.

The brown trout in the Platte weathered whirling disease a little better than the rainbows did because browns evolved in Europe along with the parasite and have some immunity, but the rainbows were devastated. They weren't entirely wiped out, however. Biologists say there's usually a small percentage of any fish population that's immune to a new disease and some researchers said that one eventual solution to whirling disease could be a naturally evolved strain of rainbows that simply didn't get it.

But the Division of Wildlife didn't want to wait for evolution and neither did fishermen, so the division began stocking rainbows in the Platte again in 1997. They used whirling disease–free wild rainbows from the Colorado River as brood stock, and planted the young trout at five inches because at that length, although they can still get and carry the parasite, their cartilage has hardened into bone so they won't be disfigured or otherwise affected.

No stocking was done in Cheesman Canyon, however, partly because it's so inaccessible, but also in large part because the canyon hadn't been hit as hard by whirling disease as the lower river. As it turned out, the "hot spot" for whirling disease spores was below the canyon, on the Wigwam Club property at the confluence with Wigwam Creek. That hot spot has since been cleaned up by the division.

The stocking of young Colorado River rainbows continued in the lower river for several years, but there's been a hiatus over the last few seasons, partly because there were enough fish in the river (at least up until the Hayman Fire) and also because the limited number of whirling disease–free trout were needed elsewhere in the state.

Fishermen still go to the South Platte, although some seem a little less enthusiastic about it now because of the perceived loss of what had become known to anglers as the South Platte strain of rainbow trout. These were brightly colored rainbows: deep green, with wide, bright red lateral stripes and iridescent gill covers. Many also had cutthroat slashes under their jaws that some said were genetic remnants of the old native greenbacks. You couldn't find prettier rainbow trout anywhere in the world.

But most of the fisheries biologists I spoke with said the South Platte strain was a romantic myth, or as one guy put it, "just fly-shop talk." They said that trout naturally take on the coloration of their environment and that any rainbow stocked in the rich, weedy South Platte would come to look like that, just as the same trout in a gray-bottomed stream would eventually turn silvery.

Since rainbows and cutthroats interbreed so readily, the cutthroat slashes could have come from anywhere at any time: from the hatcheries themselves, or from cutthroats or hybrids working down from higher up in the drainage. As early as 1918, hatchery workers described some trout from above Cheesman as "greenback and-or Yellowstone/greenback mix with rainbow contamination."

Barry Nehring did say that when fisheries biologists did genetic workups of wild rainbows from the Gunnison, Colorado and South Platte rivers, the Gunnison and Colorado fish were identical—still essentially the coastal rainbows from California that were originally stocked—but the trout from the South Platte were "genetically different." He writes that off as the result of "an incredible mishmash of stocking over the last hundred years." Nehring said the South Platte rainbows weren't an actual subspecies, but he charitably conceded that it wouldn't do any harm if fishermen wanted to think of them as a "strain," meaning, perhaps, that biologists don't much care *what* fishermen think.

On the second trip Mike and I took to the Platte that December, we met a young guy named Jesse at the trailhead into Cheesman Canyon. He was in patched waders, dressed a little too lightly for the cold weather, and was carrying a perfectly good but inexpensive rod and reel and a plastic box full of tiny little winter flies. He said he was after "those old natives," which is what some young fishermen now call the South Platte rainbows.

We wanted to talk to him because it's these young guys who often have the juju on rivers like this, especially after conditions have changed and most of us aren't back up to speed yet. He wanted to talk to *us* because it's conceivable that we'd been fishing the river on the day he was born. We reached an unspoken compromise on the hike into the canyon, with Mike and me walking a little faster than usual and Jesse apparently slowing his normal pace a bit.

We separated when Mike and I peeled off to fish the first pool above the Chutes and Jesse went on up closer to the middle of the canyon. We had our choice of water to fish because there weren't many fishermen on the river. It was cold, as I mentioned, and word was the fishing had been poor.

There didn't seem to be a lot of trout in the river, but then that's relative to the old days and also deceptive. Trout were hard to spot against the still-dark, sooty bottom and when there's nothing to get them moving, they have a way of sinking from sight anyway, only to reappear by the hundreds when a hatch comes on. There wasn't much happening in the aquatic insect department and the fish we saw were finning deep in the slower runs where they could pick off any nymphs or pupae that might drift by. They had the air about them of critters that were lying in a feeding lane simply because they didn't have anything better to do.

Some of the trout we spotted were pretty large and we did fish for them with weighted nymph rigs, but after we made a dozen casts or so—with breaks to chip ice from the guides and then warm our hands—they would slip away one by one to places where they wouldn't be bothered. On our previous trip we'd caught a few on nymphs and then a few more when there was a pulse of Blue-Winged Olive duns in early afternoon, but this time we got skunked.

Someone was required to say that it was just good to see some big rainbows still in there and Mike said it during a coffee break around three o'clock. And these would have to be rainbows that had been missed by whirling disease, survived the fire and whose ancestors hadn't seen the inside of a hatchery in half a century. A wild strain if not an actual subspecies. Those old natives.

When we got back to the trailhead that evening, there was a note from Jesse stuck under Mike's windshield wiper saying he'd caught two big 'bows on a size-26 RS-2 Emerger. Pretty much what you'd expect from a young guy who had it bad, knew the river well and who was impervious to cold and frustration.

On the walk in and the one other time we'd run into him on the river, Jesse had generously told us some of the places where he'd located big fish, and although some of the spots sounded familiar, we couldn't actually be sure where they were.

Some years ago Trout Unlimited erected a large wooden sign halfway into Cheesman Canyon on the lower trail. It shows a fairly detailed map of the river, complete with the names of pools and runs, although oddly some names were changed and others were moved from one pool to another. It doesn't make much difference, except that now you can no longer give directions to—or take them from—anyone under the age of thirty.

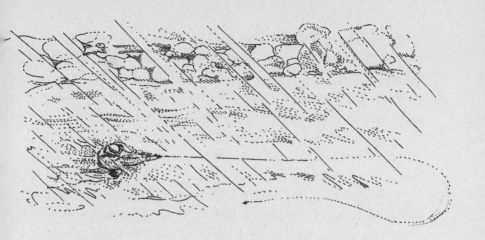

Chapter 15

WEATHER ISN'T the only thing that can go wrong on a fishing trip, but it's high on the list, which is why fishermen have an almost pathological love/hate relationship with meteorology. If there's such a thing as perfect fishing, it would require perfect weather, but in actual practice it's either too hot or too cold, too wet or too dry, too sunny or too cloudy, too windy or too still, and on those rare days when it's just right, we know it can't possibly last. Like all good comedy, fishing depends almost entirely on timing.

In February, when Mike Clark and I drove out to the Sandy River in Oregon to fish for winter steelhead, the forecast there was for rain, and that was good. The river had been low and some rain was needed to bump up the flow a little and get the fish moving. Or so they said. Mike and I are both new to steelheading, and how these fish feel about their rivers rising and falling is just one more mystery we might eventually understand with professional help.

The Sandy is a 1,200-mile drive from home: a little less than a day and a half, with a motel in Idaho on the western leg and one in Utah on the way back. We hit the first snow on the east end of Boise—a little better than halfway there—and it was snow on the passes and rain lower down the rest of the way, including a modest blizzard on Dead Man Pass in eastern Oregon, where we followed a snowplow for twenty miles and were happy to do it.

We were floating the Sandy with Mark Bachmann, who'd guided us for steelhead on the Deschutes River back in October. That trip was our first try for these big West Coast, sea-run rainbows, but with Mark's help we managed to catch a few (our first ever) and immediately developed yet another expensive and time-consuming habit, complete with new rods and reels, new flies, nonresident fishing licenses and the need to travel far from home. This is how fishermen end up broke, but happy. It seems unavoidable.

Every fisherman knows that a steelhead is a rainbow trout that acts like a salmon by being born in freshwater and then going to sea for much of its life. I'm still not sure why, though, especially since in many rivers there are identical rainbows that stay home and live out their lives in their home water. As near as I can determine, a steelhead is just a trout that wakes up one morning with a hankering to see the world. Anyone who was ever sixteen years old can understand that.

That Deschutes trip also taught us firsthand what we'd always heard about steelheading: that success is rare and fleeting, but worth the effort if you can appreciate the poetry of it. That was a completely familiar idea since I'd grown up in the Midwest, where it was believed that nothing good comes easy and, conversely, that nothing that comes easy can be all that good.

That's one of the ways that steelhead resemble Atlantic salmon and of course that's why you fish for them. Even more than their beauty, size and fight, it's the unlikelihood of catching one that makes them so sexy. Entire subcultures have developed around big sea-run fish that can just barely be caught. The English call Atlantic-salmon fishing "the sport of kings." Americans say "the best head is steelhead": different responses to the same problem, both of which breed quiet fanatics who can go for days or weeks between fish without visibly losing heart. You naturally want to catch a fish, but it's that world-weary patience you aspire to.

I had a brief flirtation with Atlantic-salmon fishing years ago, but it didn't take, even though I liked almost everything about it: the rivers, the talk, the fat books by stuffy English writers, the fish themselves (the few I saw, plus the larger idea of them), the rods, the flies and even the long aristocratic history of the sport that you could take seriously or not, depending on how you felt that day. Even the nose-in-the-air snootiness of it could be amusing as long as you kept your distance.

The only thing I didn't like was the price tag. After a few tries, I began to suspect that doing it well on good water would end up costing me a fortune, and then on an obscure, mediocre salmon river in New Brunswick a kindly old salmon fisherman confirmed that. "If you want to pay twenty times what this is costing for the best weeks on the best rivers," he said, "you can catch all the bloody salmon you want." I understood this might not be true in every case, but it would be true enough in the long run, and since fishing had already come close to bankrupting me a few times, I just couldn't see upping the ante.

But steelhead are more accessible in every way if you live

here in the northern Colorado Rockies. Starting from home before dawn, I can drive to some steelhead rivers in a long day, and a hell of a lot more in two days. Three days behind the wheel can put me on some of the best steelhead water in the world. Once there I can stay in cheap motels, or maybe camp, and fish free public water. Beyond that, it's just time, and thank God I still have more time than money. You can drive yourself to tears of frustration just as easily with steelhead as with Atlantic salmon, but you can do it at blue-collar prices.

And I have to say that the idea of driving somewhere to fish, always my first choice anyway, had gotten even more attractive recently. On that trip to the Deschutes in October, four of us had flown from Denver to Portland, then rented a car to drive back east a few hours to the little town of Maupin to meet our guides. The travel alone had cost us each the price of a good fly rod and had been the usual nightmare of long waits, bad food, surly service and oppressive security.

We'd shipped our long Spey rods and sleeping bags ahead with UPS to keep the airline from sending them to Hawaii by mistake, but we carried on shorter tubes with our shorter three-piece rods. At the security checkpoint we were told we couldn't take them on because pool cues were considered weapons, and it was more complicated than you'd imagine convincing them that fly rods and pool cues were two entirely different things.

Apparently the pool-cue thing was in the air somehow, because by the time that trip was over at least a dozen people had said to me, "I didn't think you could bring pool cues on a plane" or, "Going to play pool, huh?" Half a lifetime as a fishing writer and I was being mistaken for a hustler. On the flight back from Portland a woman next to me looked at my battered, water-stained rod case and said, "Well, whatever you're doing, you obviously do a lot of it." I said, "Yes, ma'am."

I'm not arguing with the necessity for heightened security and if I were in charge, I, too, would be paranoid and suspicious. I'd also arrange to be as capricious as possible in order to keep the bad guys off balance. It's just that as a passenger you have to ask yourself, Is it worth spending all that hard-earned money for the privilege of presenting yourself as a suspect and being treated like dirt? More and more now I'm thinking, No. Not when I can take an extra day and just drive.

But then there are people who seem to thrive on air travel, as well as the wheeled luggage, beepers, cell phones and other accoutrements that go with it. I see them on every trip, always in a hurry and always frowning, but always breezing through the same bottlenecks where I get stuck. They probably foreshadow our next evolutionary step. They won't become creatures of pure thought as happens on *Star Trek*; they'll be creatures of pure stress.

Things looked good that first day on the Sandy River. The water was clear, Mark said the flow was right, and I'd been practicing with the big fourteen-foot, two-handed Spey rod, so I was getting the casts out well enough—at least while I was alone. If I knew or even suspected that I was being watched, I'd begin to blow casts out of self-consciousness, but Mark said that's not peculiar to rookies. He said you can make the best caster in the world screw up just by staring at him. I've tried that a few times since, and it seems to be true.

But then casting difficulties are just the first awkward step in any new kind of fishing. As Chris said of Spey casting, "It's fun to be doing something new, but it's annoying to be a beginner again after all these years."

I also have a lot to learn about playing big, hot fish on a fourteen-foot, two-handed rod. Virtually all casting instruction ends at the moment you hook a fish. With steelhead, that's like teaching a new driver how to start a car and then turning him loose in rush-hour traffic.

But at its best, steelhead fishing is meditational. There's the elaborately graceful Spey cast, the big upstream mend, the shape of the line on the water that makes the fly swing across the current, but slower than the current, like a strong but lazy fish. You start at the head of a long run, fish out the cast, take two steps downstream and do it again, and then again and again until you come to the end. An hour can go by, during which you won't have a single coherent thought.

Mark had the boat (a sturdy hand-made pontoon job with rod holders made of irrigation pipe) and of course he knew where to fish. He fishes and guides on other steelhead rivers, but he's fished the Sandy for over thirty years and has literally written the book on it: the Sandy River installment of the *Steelhead River Journal* series from Frank Amato Publications.

I can tell you that having written a book simply means that you wrote a book, but it was clear Mark knew his stuff after our first day on the Deschutes back in October as things went smoothly with no apparent effort on his part. For instance, I do a double Spey cast much better right-handed than left-handed, and toward evening of the first day I thought how lucky it was for me that almost every good run Mark put me on was on the right side of the river. But then, was it really just luck?

And of course he eventually managed to get some rank beginners into their first steelhead, which is no mean feat. A lifetime of fishing experience does help when it comes to new tackle and a new species, but it doesn't always help as much as you might have hoped. It's a guide's job to try to isolate the one or two elements that could put a duffer in the zone, while leaving the subtleties for another time.

Mark also summed up the science of guiding as succinctly as I've ever heard it done. He said, "Guiding is easy: you just substitute the word *please* for the word *asshole,* as in, 'Fish here, please' or, 'Get in the boat now, please.'" Up until then, I just thought he was being polite.

It rained constantly on the Sandy and it was pretty chilly, but that was just fine. We were dressed for it, the fish like it and it made the river beautiful with wet colors and banks of cloud obscuring the rim of the canyon. In this stretch the Sandy flows through primeval-looking rain forest with tall trees, giant ferns and moss on every permanent surface: the kind of thick, dripping temperate jungle where you felt that if you stood still too long you'd end up covered in mushrooms.

By comparison, the lower Deschutes had been entirely familiar: a dry canyon in October covered with bare rock, grass and scrub, the weather cool and bright—a little too bright for steelhead, they said—with a narrow band of alder and hackberry along the water. Just enough trees and in just the right place to hamper a back cast, hence the Spey rods that allow for an eighty-foot roll cast with no more than a rod's length of room behind you. The Deschutes could have been any one of a hundred trout rivers back home, except that it was three or four times wider and its fish had recently been in the Pacific Ocean, possibly as far west as the Sea of Japan. (Chris once said that when you hook a steelhead, you can feel the ocean in it. I thought that was nicely put.) The florid, fog-shrouded Sandy was a lot smaller and less intimidating than the Deschutes. It was also more like what I'd imagined about steelheading when I knew nothing at all, but tried to picture it.

In that first full dawn-to-dusk day on the Sandy, we each got several tugs. I got a pretty big steelhead right to the beach before he threw the hook and escaped, and Mark landed one and lost another. All in all, it was a better-than-average day of steelhead fishing and I learned more about the cast, mend and drift from watching Mark fish than I had when he was guiding us on the Deschutes, standing on the bank trying to tell us how to do it.

We fished large tube flies on sink-tip lines. Four months previously on the Deschutes we'd fished small wets on floating lines, at least in the mornings and evenings. Apparently that's the seasonal difference. In a very general way, it's small and shallow in the fall, big and deep in the winter. This makes a kind of instinctive sense.

These tube flies were brilliantly simple: marabou and a few strands of tinsel wound on a 1 1/2-inch-long plastic tube that was then strung down the leader onto a short-shanked hook. The stubby hook gives the fish less leverage than a long shank and is therefore more likely to hold, and the whole rig also amounts to a large fly that's nonetheless almost weightless, so it's easier to cast. I'd always wondered what the deal was with tube flies. Now I know.

The favorite tube-fly colors on the Sandy were red and orange and black and blue. Mark said they probably mimicked squid getting excited and turning bright colors or getting scared and squirting ink, two things steelhead would key on in the open ocean. I love hearing theories about flies. True or not, they always sound so good.

The strikes were different, too. On the Deschutes, you'd hold under your index finger a shock loop of line that you were supposed to feed to the fish when you felt the strike, giving him enough time and slack to turn and take the hook in the corner of the jaw. But the strikes were violent, and if you were half asleep—as you could easily be after hours of methodical casting—the fish would take the fly, pull out the loop, hit the drag of the reel and be hooked before any of it registered. All that was left to do was say "Oh, shit" and hang on.

On the Sandy, in the winter, in the rain, the takes were hesitant: more the tick-tick-tick you'd get from a bluegill worrying a nymph than the slam you expect from a steelhead. I just stood there through the first two not knowing what else to do. On the third, I fed the loop at the first tick, set when the line came tight and had the fish. It was heartbreaking to lose him right at my feet, but I'd hooked him and felt I'd learned something. This was still early in the romance, when each day brings new discoveries because you still know next to nothing.

It rained all that first day, sometimes hard, sometimes just enough to keep everything good and wet. It rained all that night and it was still raining when we got on the water the next morning. The river didn't exactly have trees and barns floating in it, but it was up and rising, the water was cloudy and since things were less than perfect, the fish were not pleased.

In one deep run we strung up the heaviest sink-tip any of us had and took turns trying to Spey-cast it. Even Mark had some trouble with this depth charge, but when he finally hit the slot, he caught a bright, twelve-pound steelhead. Mike had gotten a halfhearted tug an hour earlier, and I never had a touch. At one point Mark said to me, in the diplomatic way even off-duty guides have, "You're starting to look like a real steelhead fisherman." I hoped he meant my casting, but he might have been referring to the blank stare.

That evening we checked with the guy at Mark's fly shop in Welches, who said things looked grim. The river had been almost too high to fish that day and the forecast was for more hard rain with no end in sight. He said, "If it snows above 4,000 feet tonight, you might just stand a chance. If it rains, you're screwed."

It rained hard through the night and the next morning we were, indeed, screwed. The Sandy was blown out and, according to the all-knowing, all-seeing computer in the shop, so were all the nearby rivers that had runs of steelhead. It would be days before any river came down enough to fish even if it stopped raining. It *would* stop eventually, but there was no telling when.

There were big smiles all around. If you can't see the humor in a busted fishing trip, you're in the wrong sport, and of course to be a real steelheader you need an entire repertoire of stories just like this, so you might as well get started.

With nothing else to do, Mike and I packed up and set out on the twenty-some-hour drive home. As it turned out, all but the last few miles of it would be in rain or snow. That naturally caused some problems like poor visibility and questionable traction, both of which slowly but surely rattle your nerves.

The best way to travel in the West is on back roads and in no particular hurry, but the interstates are just too tempting on long trips because of the speeds you can achieve. It's true that for engineering reasons these highways aren't built through the most spectacular country, but the ride can still be pleasant if you appreciate emptiness and don't let your attention wander too much. You try to relax and enjoy the view without forgetting that you're hurtling along at dangerous speeds and could go fatally out of control at any second. You easily fall into this model of American culture in which movement is good (and the faster the better) while stopping or even slowing down for icy roads is bad. In fact, on most interstates, stopping just to stop is illegal.

But although it gave us some trouble, we were happy to see precipitation of any kind after three years of drought, and especially pleased to see that the storm had slid over the Continental Divide into eastern Wyoming and on south into Colorado where, as it turned out, it would snow hard for the next several days. It was fun to think that we'd been with this weather in Oregon and that it had followed us home like an enormous puppy. We'd violated the first rule of driving trips whereby you should always spend more time fishing than traveling, but this time that was just part of the adventure.

Fishermen have been known to complain, joke or brag about the abysmal boredom of steelhead fishing, but it's nothing compared to a day and a half's worth of driving with bad weather, bad roads, bad food, gut-wrenching coffee, excessive speed, suicidal truck drivers, sore backs and poor radio reception, with nothing much to talk about except the next steelhead trip. All the way home, we wished we were back on the river. It was more fun than it sounds.

Chapter 16

OSAGE COUNTY, Oklahoma, is roughly six hundred miles from where I live in the foothills of northern Colorado. To get there you drive east and south on interstates, U.S. and state highways, paved and gravel county roads, and then two-rut dirt tracks to finally get to the fishing. You can do it in just under twelve hours if you don't dawdle, break down or hit weather. That much windshield time can leave you feeling like you might cough up a hair ball, but you can recover from moderate road burn with a single night's sleep, and the cost in gas is a fraction of what you'd pay to park at an airport for a week, never mind the plane ticket. As trips go, it's a nice, neat bite out of time and space.

The countryside changes gradually on the long drive from the Rocky Mountains as you simultaneously lose altitude and latitude until you're finally in a new kind of place altogether: a place far from small, cold trout streams and pine trees, where there are yellow-billed cuckoos in the signature Osage orange trees and scissor-tailed flycatchers perched on the telephone wires; a place where the distinctive regional hazards include buffalo mites, chiggers, water moccasins and twisters.

That's another reason to travel: Around home I know the birds and trees well enough that I often just note their presence without actually looking at them, and I also know what potential dangers to watch out for—mostly my own clumsiness, plus the occasional rattlesnake or mountain lion. But on the road every new leaf and birdsong grabs your attention, especially if you're driving alone with the radio off and the windows down. Between complicated reveries and worrying about the ancient truck you're driving, you see the new place in a way you haven't seen home since your first week there.

There's even a different dialect of the language as you get down into rural Oklahoma, with a few unfamiliar expressions and a hard drawl that's part southern, part western. It's entirely intelligible with only the occasional misunderstanding, as when a man talked about the fine new tires he had on his land. Turns out he meant "towers"—elevated stands for deer hunting.

In the first full week of May, Oklahoma was a good six weeks ahead of Colorado. The grass was already tall and lush. Hardwood trees were fully leafed out and had gone from the pale chartreuse of new growth to the hard green of mature leaves. The air was warm and humid and downright hot the few times the sun came out and the wind died. It was an unsettled spring at the height of bass, panfish and tornado season.

I'd gone south in part to escape the runoff at home that had the streams and rivers too high and muddy to fish for the first time in three years. It was wonderful to see the old spring floods return, but during all those seasons of drought we'd gotten used to fishing dry flies in clear streams in April and May, and so a kind of restlessness had set in along with the high water.

The drought couldn't have broken more dramatically that winter if it had been scripted by a Hollywood screenwriter. The storm that followed Mike and me home from Oregon in February had been one of several pretty good ones, and the snowpack was looking better than it had in quite a while, although at that time it was still lower than normal.

But then in early March, A.K. and I were planning to go fish the Cheesman Canyon stretch of the South Platte River to get a jump on the coming season. The river was still in low winter flows, so the fishing would be a little ticklish, but the forecast had predicted what looked like promising early spring fishing weather with an approaching low-pressure front, chilly but not too cold temperatures, overcast skies and maybe some light snow or drizzle. It sounded perfect for a midge hatch or maybe the early Blue-Winged Olive mayflies that had been coming off a few weeks earlier than usual over the last few years.

It did stay on the warm side, but I wasn't prepared for a pounding blizzard with snow depths over a few days of three and four feet in the foothills and upwards of six to nine feet in parts of the high country—and neither was the rest of the Front Range. Everything from Fort Collins to Denver and west to Utah was shut down for days: roads, interstates, schools, city governments, Meals on Wheels, you name it. Limbs piled with wet snow fell on power lines and blacked out whole communities, especially those in what they call "outlying areas." The press named it "The Blizzard of '03" and covered it like a blanket. (In America, there's always enough electricity to broadcast interviews with people who are freezing in kitchens filled with rotting food because their power has been out for a week.) Of course people kept warm in whatever ways they could and, as you'd expect, nine months later in some areas record numbers of babies were born.

A.K. and I didn't even bother calling each other to cancel the trip. It's about an eighty-mile drive from here to the South Platte, and although the fishing probably would have been good, all the roads were closed, so we'd have had to make the trip on snowshoes.

If you don't count people without electricity or the stranded travelers who had to camp at Denver International Airport for three days, I don't remember hearing any complaints. All anyone wanted that winter was something like a normal snowpack. Few of us expected to get most of it dumped in our laps in three days, but if that's how it wanted to happen, fine.

The Blizzard of '03 pushed the snowpack in the state's river drainages well past 100 percent—including the enormous South Platte drainage where I and most of my fishing friends live—and it was the first shot in a long, wet spring. By mid April it was still raining or snowing pretty regularly (depending on the altitude) and the cottonwoods, cliff rose and mountain mahogany around my house were as green as I'd ever seen them. The freestone rivers and streams were blown out and unfishable, and, as feared, there were flash floods on the South Platte around the Hayman burn that sent slugs of silt down the river. But, by all accounts, the mud wasn't quite the consistency of wet cement and no trout were seen swimming out on the banks to escape it. It was hoped that the floods had flushed the soot from the river without replacing it with enough sediment to smother the vegetation and the mayflies that live on it. When things settled down, there'd have to be yet another trip to the river to see how the poor old girl was doing.

It was truly a different kind of year. The north and south forks of the modest, harmless little St. Vrain Creek that's my nearest home water were closed to "recreational activity" for the first time in anyone's memory. A kayaker drowned on the Cache la Poudre River just north of here, and two fishermen were killed, one by lightning, the other in a landslide.

In early June, Trailridge Road—a forty-five minute drive from here and the highest paved road in the U.S. at 12,183 feet—was still closed because of snow. On June 8, the first anniversary of the start of the Hayman Fire on the South Platte, there was a hard frost.

Of course we didn't know it then, but it would have been at about the height of the floods that the water districts, sensing a perception problem, were producing a multimillion-dollar series of TV commercials warning that the drought wasn't over and that we should still be scared as hell and, by implication, that we should trust them implicitly. One of the ads showed a rotting rowboat beached on the cracked bottom of a dried-up lake, at a time when the state's reservoirs were up to 80 percent of capacity and filling fast and the rivers were still running too high to fish. And that was it: an ad apparently selling nothing, not unlike those commercials pumping a new drug without saying what the drug is for. You know something more is coming and if you gave it some thought you could probably guess what.

Oddly enough, at around that same time the TV news started running similar stories saying that experts were warning us not to be fooled by all this water; that the drought hadn't really ended. The "experts," of course, were the water providers for whom water is money, so naturally there can never be enough. It was possible to suspect collusion when the news story was immediately followed by a commercial saying exactly the same thing. (For the record, reporting that cites a single position from a single, self-interested source isn't journalism. At best, it's laziness; at worst, it's propaganda.) It was one of those times when the world you see on TV and in the newspapers is not the one you see outside your back door, so you have to wonder, Who's wrong?

Toward the end of this snow job, the water providers formally asked the state legislature for two billion dollars for unspecified water projects to be built at unspecified times and places. Never mind what it's for, just give us the money. Of course. Should have seen that one coming.

But all those shenanigans were still months in the future when, not knowing what to expect, I packed up enough bass tackle to outfit three fishermen and left for Oklahoma to fish with three locals: Steve Huston, Dennis Tatum and Gene Holland. I'd met these guys a few months earlier when they came to Colorado to talk to Mike Clark, the bamboo-rod maker. We'd hit it off, agreeing about bass, bluegills, bamboo fly rods and a few other important things, while carefully staying away from politics so as not to pointlessly muddy the water. One night at dinner I'd picked their brains about rumors of good warm-water fly-fishing in Oklahoma that was largely unknown outside the state and they'd invited me down to see for myself. It was as painless as that.

It turns out the rumors were pretty much true. This is rolling, mostly open country with scattered hardwood groves in the low spots, and the occasional hill high enough to offer a big, sprawling view. There are a few large public reservoirs and hundreds of smaller, more obscure ranch ponds, many of which are tucked in draws a long way from public roads and below the line of sight, so they're nicely hidden. It seems as though every likely-looking gully has been dammed for reasons anyone with thirsty cows or a fishing pole can understand.

Some ponds are fairly new or newly dredged out; others are so old the dams were built by hand with the help of mules and have since merged with the landscape and gone wild. The limestone geology makes the ponds as weedy and rich in bugs as English chalk streams, and virtually all of them have been stocked with largemouth bass, panfish and sometimes catfish.

Like much of the western ranch country, a lot of the fishing here is beyond the reach of an outsider. You'd have to trespass brazenly even to find most of the ponds, and then look longer and harder to locate someone to ask for permission to fish. Even then, a moderately reasonable landowner could glance at your dopey fishing hat and out-of-state plates and politely say no. It's not exactly exclusionary (fences are there to keep cattle in, not to keep fishermen out), it's just that the fishing is there for whom it's for, while the rest of us are out of the loop. It's always been like that. It's nothing personal.

My benefactors had access to some of this stuff by virtue of being local fishermen and therefore part of the web of favors, friendship, business, sport and family history that makes a rural community coherent. I was along for the ride and only got hints of it all in the course of things. For instance, Dennis was part of a lease on a big handful of good ponds that was amazingly cheap: less per year than you'd pay for a single day of guided float fishing on a western trout river. (Everyone admires good fishing, but here the big bucks go for rights to hunt white-tailed deer, wild turkeys and quail.) And Steve used to run a local funeral home, so, as he put it, he had buried many old ranchers and now fishes with permission from their widows and children.

Our mornings would begin with a stop at the warehouse. These guys are serious fishermen and they had all reached the point where they had more gear than their houses would hold and their wives would tolerate, so they'd gone together and rented a small old tin industrial building down by the tracks where they stored an impressive collection of rods, reels, fly boxes, trailered boats, float tubes, pontoon boats, waders, flippers, cases of bottled water and I don't know what all else. Leaning against one wall was a handsome wood coffin with brass fittings, presumably a leftover of Steve's that might eventually come in handy.

Then we'd head to a cafe with a dirt parking lot full of pickups, where the food was good and cheap and there was lots of it. The pickups were American-made and well used. The bumper stickers were religious, patriotic or both, since here in America the two invariably go hand in hand.

I'd quickly realized that this was the kind of place where a guy with liberal tendencies should probably stay quiet about certain subjects, not for the sake of safety, but just so as not to needlessly poison the atmosphere. I mean, you can honestly disagree with people about things like God and the Republican Party, but you can't change their minds. You can, however, really strain their natural sense of hospitality.

But that's not to say that the place was particularly straight-laced. Inside the cafe, one of the locals wore an extra-large T-shirt that said, "Holy Cow Beer: Helping Ugly People Have Sex for Over 20 Years." The waitress was efficient and good-looking, wearing one of those bare-midriff tops. When she turned her back after taking your order, you could see part of an elaborate tattoo that seemed to be crawling out of her low-slung jeans. She'd catch you looking and give you that over-the-shoulder grin that said, Go ahead and wonder, cowboy, 'cause you'll never get to see it.

We spent our days pond hopping, fishing mostly from float tubes and pontoon boats because those were all we needed on the small ponds and because there were no boat ramps anyway. The wind blew constantly, which sometimes made casting and paddling a belly boat difficult, but the weather was warm and humid, the water was choppy enough to cover your cast and the sky was usually cloudy, which is known to be a prescription for good fishing.

I learned to keep an eye out for water moccasins that could be hard to see swimming through the choppy water. The rattlesnakes back home are also potentially dangerous, but on the whole they're shy, secretive critters that don't want trouble. Moccasins, on the other hand, can be pretty aggressive, so it's best to give them a generous right of way. Once, while bass fishing in a pond in south Texas, a moccasin had tried to crawl up on my float tube, probably thinking it was a convenient island. I tried to scare him away, but only succeeded in pissing him off. It was the only time I've ever used a fly rod as a weapon.

My friends said the bass fishing was actually a little slow, probably because spring itself had come on a little late that year, just like back home, and the water was still a little too cool. There were stories of bass weighing eight or nine pounds coming from these ponds, but I knew what that meant. I had recently told someone that a certain small stream near home held brown trout to sixteen inches, but I failed to mention that I had caught precisely one trout of that size on the rare perfect day after thirty years of hard fishing.

It's true there were some dead spells (when are there not dead spells in fishing?) but we caught bass every day, sometimes pretty nice ones weighing a few pounds. Some came to the big size-4 deer-hair diving frogs I like, but the boys were doing better on smaller flies, so I switched.

I think it's to my credit that I'm now usually unaware of competition with other fishermen when I'm up. When I'm down, I'm aware of it only in the most neutral sense: That guy is catching more fish than I am. It looks like fun. I'd like to catch more fish, too. Plus, a stranger who doesn't try to copy what the locals are doing probably has too much to prove for his own good.

It was when I changed to another favorite pattern, a size-8 cork-pencil popper that I see as a cross between a baby frog and a dragonfly, that I started getting into the big sunfish. As it turned out, the panfishing was exceptional enough to make me forget about bass entirely for hours at a time. There were white crappies, black crappies, bluegills, green sunfish, bluegill-green hybrids, rock bass, red ears and long ears. They came in the usual wide range of sizes, but the biggest were close to a pound: a big handful side-on and wide across the part that passes for shoulders on a fish.

Dennis said the biggest fish were all green-bluegill hybrids, and that's what I thought, too, but I have to admit that when sunfish start to crossbreed, my identifications can get fuzzy. These fish were mostly dark greenish-bronze overall with a slight iridescent cast that doesn't show up in the snapshots. Some shaded to pale yellow on the bellies, but others didn't. The fins on some were a plain translucent olive, while others had muddy yellowish or orange margins. But they all had those midnight-blue, thumb-shaped gill flaps that gave them the name bluegill.

A few of mine came from open water, but most were in potholes in the thick weeds closer to shore, where you'd look for bass. I got some bass in this stuff, too (since they liked the smaller bugs anyway), and in the first few seconds of a fight—before he snarled you in weeds and you had to go dig him out by hand—the biggest bluegills felt the same as bass weighing three times more. In open water I could tell the difference. With room to move, a sunfish planes strongly off at an angle like a lopsided saucer. When you get a real big one, it's like trying to land a Frisbee sideways.

A few days into the trip it became obvious that the bass would bite best when there were tornadoes around, and that happened often that week. One day, something like eighty tornadoes tore through the countryside (a new record, they said). There were enough tornadoes around that if you stood in one spot, you'd eventually see a few; if not the funnels themselves, then at least the black walls of the cells that spawned them.

The weather that whole week was a constant buzz. Every radio or TV I came close to was tuned to weather and the coverage was wall-to-wall. There were detailed forecasts; weather maps showing bright, multicolored blobs marching across the state; film clips of wreckage; interviews with survivors. In the evenings you'd read about the weather in the newspaper. Driving out to fish, Steve had recordings from the National Weather Service on his shortwave. As if all that weren't enough, you could also spend an inordinate amount of time staring at the sky.

On the stormiest afternoon, we were fishing a beautiful big

pond littered with the kind of flooded timber that bass seem to love. To get there we'd gone off-road on faint tire tracks and then off-off-road to bounce down a long grassy hill in low-range four-wheel. You had to think the place hadn't been fished much. The wind was whipping and the sky was dark, but we were accustomed to that and had gotten used to cutting it close.

I had paddled my float tube up a flooded creek mouth with lots of cover and a strip of smooth water along a high bank that cut the wind. Out in the open, you had to cast with the wind or not at all, even with the long, nine-weight bass rod I'd strung up. But in that creek channel the bass were lying within inches of the steep bank, in the narrow strip of calm water, and they were wound tight. Most strikes came within a second or two of the fly hitting the water, before the ripples had a chance to spread. The rest came on the first pull.

By then I'd learned that when the weather got this threatening, I should switch back to the size-4 deer-hair bug because the bass that had been fastidiously sipping little poppers on a faint twitch would now suddenly explode on something big and juicy and moving fast.

These were bigger bass than the biggest ones I'd caught up till then—not the eight- and nine-pounders of local legend, but longer, heavier and stronger. Maybe this was just an exceptional pond, or maybe these big boys had been pouting until the barometric pressure crashed, causing them to think that the next frog that swam by could be their last meal. Of course none of this was a complete surprise. A friend once asked me why I keep going into tornado country during tornado season. I had to say it's because that's when the bass are biting.

There was a period of time—I can't say how long—when

these fish were all but jumping onto the apron of my belly boat. I fell into the easy confidence you feel when the fishing gets furious and missing one is nothing because you'll get another pull in two or three more casts. For a while I was getting bass or missing strikes often enough to keep my attention off the weather, but finally I could no longer deny that the air had turned a sort of sickly green color. The sky had gone black and the thunder had not only gotten closer and louder, but the rumbles had run together into a constant roar that sounded like a jet engine. I glanced over my shoulder and saw that my three friends had already gotten out of the water and were quickly dragging their float tubes up the hill toward the trucks. They'd probably yelled at me, but the wind and the thunder were loud and I was clear across the pond.

Anyway, I reeled in, paddled quickly out of the creek mouth and got out of the water. We threw our stuff in the two pickups and dashed for the main road as well as you can dash on two faint, bumpy tire tracks through the grass. Steve's shortwave crackled with static and I couldn't make out what was being said, although the computer-generated robot voice sounded reassuringly calm.

Sheets of rain and hail hit us before we made the gravel road and it got dark enough to turn on the headlights, but the ground didn't get slippery enough to bog us down. A few miles farther on, the sun broke out and it seemed as though nothing had happened except that the road was six inches deep in muddy water moving at a moderate current. Steve called home on his cell phone to see if everything was okay. It was.

We learned later that that particular tornado had passed over Fairfax Lake a half mile away, where a man named Jamie

Flegler was fishing alone. We talked to him at a restaurant the next night and he still seemed shaken, his eyes darting around the room as if he thought the tornado was still out there looking for him and might come through a window at any second. He said he had also stayed on the water too long, but when he saw the funnel coming toward him across the small lake, he drove his boat full speed onto the bank and dove into a ditch, where he held onto handfuls of grass and chanted "Oh my God, oh my God" as the storm passed directly over him. His boat was dinged up, but he wasn't hurt except for a bruise on his ribs where he'd landed on a rock when he dove into the ditch.

He said he also remembered the bass biting like crazy, right up until the moment he saw the funnel come over the dam.

The night of that particular tornado, we went into Ponca City to eat dinner at a sports bar where all the televisions were tuned to the weather, and as we drove through the town's wet streets I noticed once again how many churches there were. There seemed to be one or two on every block. There were as many churches as there are restaurants in Boulder, Colorado, where a food critic for the *Daily Camera* once said that if every man, woman and child in town decided to go out for dinner at the same moment, there'd be seats for all of them. But then it may not be entirely coincidental that Tornado Alley is also the Bible Belt.

Chapter 17

IT HAPPENED gradually, as these things do, but there was a single moment when it was clear that it *had* happened. I think it was in our fourth consecutive year of fishing the Nebraska Sand Hills for largemouth bass. On the last morning of that trip, Ed and I walked over to the office of the little fish camp where we'd been staying to check out of our tiny cabin, reserve another one for the following year and to formally say goodbye to Skeeter, the camp dog. Skeeter is a West Highland white terrier (what you might call a white Scottie) who would have been fourteen that year—a little slow, a little hard of hearing, but otherwise okay. Still, fourteen is ancient for a dog, and when you were ready to leave, there was the thought that you might not see old Skeeter again.

The daughter of the woman who runs the place was behind the counter, and when she flipped open the big reservation book, she said, "You're Ed and John, right?"

"Right."

"Well, Jeri already has you down. Same week next June. That okay?"

"Yeah," we said in unison. "That's okay."

So we had officially become regulars, automatically booked for the same week until we said otherwise, and the timing seemed about right, since we'd finally gotten comfortable with the fishing there and even somewhat knowledgeable about it, at least at that one time of year.

Looking back on it, the whole thing had progressed by a route that should be predictable to any fisherman. At first we'd gone there just to check it out as yet another place we'd never been that was supposed to be good. (So far, at least, there are more of these just in North America than you'll ever even hear about, let alone get to, but you have to make a stab at it.) More often than not, these are one-time trips, but we'd liked this new water enough to come back the next year and then the year after that, simultaneously exploring and enjoying a growing sense of familiarity. Eventually, the question of coming back the next year became a foregone conclusion. Jeri, the owner of the camp, saw that this was becoming a tradition with us and that was okay with her. Whatever she may have thought of us as human beings, we were quiet, polite, we left the cabin clean and our checks cleared. What else could you ask for?

I think we liked this place as much for its feeling of permanence as for the good fishing. On one of the early trips, Ed had said, with undisguised admiration, that he'd bet the camp hadn't changed since the 1950s except maybe for the odd coat of paint or new doorknob. On our most recent trip, I was talking to a woman who was there with her husband and two kids. She pointed to her daughter, who must have been about six, and said, "I started coming here with my folks when I was her age and I haven't missed a year since." I guessed that would date her first trip to more like the late 1960s than the '50s, but it was close enough. I asked her if the place had changed much. She glanced around and said, "No, not much." So there you have it: the testimony of an eyewitness. Things like that are important to Ed and me since we're among those who spent the first half of our lives wanting things to change and are now spending the rest wanting what's left to stay the same.

My trip to Oklahoma for bass had come just before our seventh year of fishing the Sand Hills. It's not that I'd gotten tired of the place, I'd just been bitten by the wanderlust for different bass in different water—sort of the angling version of what married men call "the seven-year itch." I liked Oklahoma for all the reasons I mentioned earlier (not the least of which was not getting killed by a tornado) but when we headed back to Nebraska less than a month later, I felt an old faithfulness kick in, even though I was still scratching three-week-old Oklahoma chigger bites.

These Nebraska lakes had been a little intimidating at first, as new water can be when there's almost too much of it. There were lots of lakes in the area, ranging in size from small ones between about fifty and eighty acres to some whoppers that covered nearly eight hundred acres and looked big enough to have tides. They were all close enough together and accessible enough that any morning over breakfast you could decide to fish any one of them, and if one lake was a bust, you could trailer up the john boat and be on another one in less than an hour.

That turned out to be a mixed blessing. When there's just one lake, you commit: poking around, trying different spots and different tactics, gutting out the doldrums and then bearing down in the evening. You know that any good water at the right time of year is likely to give up some fish eventually unless something out of your control is just off, and that could be anything from the wrong water temperature to your own ineptness.

When there are lots of lakes and moving is so easy, you can cut your losses, but you can also lose patience before you've given a place a fair shake, momentarily forgetting that patience is a fisherman's only known virtue. (I still remember my grandmother explaining to me that God usually sees to it that you have enough, but when you try for more, you often end up with nothing.) I remember one day when we got out early and launched on three different lakes before dusk. We wondered later if we'd allowed ourselves to panic, but then it was that third lake that finally gave up a few good bass, so maybe it was just dedication.

By now we've fished almost all the lakes in the area and have settled on some favorites. We like the small lakes because their size makes them seem friendlier and because we've caught lots of bass on them, including some of our biggest. The larger lakes can also fish well, but they're more mysterious, as if the bass sometimes get lost out in all that water and can't find their way back to where they're supposed to be. The big water can also be more dangerous when weather comes up suddenly. You can find yourself a long way out, pushing waves and a headwind with a 36-pound-thrust electric trolling motor that seems inadequate.

But then you fish the cover when you're looking for bass, so all that water usually just amounts to distance you have to run the boat across to reach the islands of reeds where these fish hang out most dependably. From a distance, these islands look like dry land covered with tall grass, but they're actually patches of bamboo-like common reeds standing in water several feet deep, with their trunks making a sunken forest where frogs, baitfish and bass like to lurk.

You start by casting to the outside edges, trying to put your deer-hair bug so close it touches the stalks. When bass are really wired, they'll move a long way for a bug, but then at other times they'll get so comfortably tucked into their weed beds that if they have to so much as poke their heads out in the open, they won't eat.

The accuracy of your cast makes a huge difference and is an obvious mark of skill. I remember a friend telling me about the time he was out with an old bass fisherman he wanted to impress. He was casting his fly to within six inches of the heaviest cover and not getting any strikes. Finally the old fisherman said, "If all you're gonna do is fish open water, we might as well go home."

After you've fished the edges of the weeds, you carefully pole your boat into the cover, casting to the channels, bays and potholes. In theory, any place you can get your fly to hit the water could draw a strike. In practice, the tighter spots often leave your bass bug dangling helplessly a foot above the surface, and although half the fishing magazine covers from the last century show bass leaping up to grab dangling lures, that seldom actually happens.

There are a couple of reed islands on one of the bigger lakes that we like a lot. The water is deeper here than it is in some, so the reeds aren't packed so tightly and there's a little more room to cast. Not only that, but there are days when bass and sometimes also yard-long pike crowd into these things, looking for food or at least not above ambushing something that looks edible.

We almost always fish floating deer-hair bugs in these lakes because they usually work and because it's so sweet to see the fish whack them on the surface. But one day at these islands we couldn't buy a strike on top, so we tried five-inch-long rabbit-strip leeches with lead eyeballs—the fly fisher's answer to the rubber worm.

That did it. We caught bass all morning, and some were bigger than what we were used to in that spot: as much as two pounds heavier, with mouths you could stick a fist in. We burned film taking hero shots of each other holding bass and thought we'd learned the trick, but it didn't work the next day and it has never worked the same way since. It was just one of those things that happen to fishermen who put in their time, but otherwise, as they say in the Midwest, "It's a head-scratcher."

On the second day of our last trip we tried that spot again, but the lake was in the middle of an algae bloom so thick it was like fishing in split-pea soup. We gave it a chance, but the visibility was so poor that a bright red and yellow bunny leech would sink out of sight in two inches of water.

Eventually we got the boat out, moved to one of the smaller lakes where the water was clear and caught some bass before dark. It took an hour of prospecting, but we figured out that the fish were not only tight to the weeds, but also tight to the banks, in the places where, if you were wading, you'd plant your foot one last time before stepping up onto dry land. When they came, the strikes were instantaneous, as if there were some chemical reaction that made your deer-hair frog explode the second it came in contact with water.

I caught two good-sized bass and then offered to switch off on the oars with Ed. He glanced at the dusky sky and said, "Go ahead, man. It's your night." I got one more before dark.

The big lake full of algae had been almost vacant that day, but there were several boats on the small one and all the trailers on shore had Nebraska plates. But then it wouldn't be right if the locals weren't already there before the tourists caught up.

This lake was brim full the last time we fished it and that was good to see. Over the previous three years, the area had suffered from the same drought that had hit the northern Colorado Rockies back home so hard, and the lakes had begun to shrink. It was almost imperceptible at first, especially on the biggest ones, but eventually there were reeds and cattails ten feet up the banks that had once stood in several feet of water and some of the rough boat ramps had almost doubled in length. Plenty of the changes back home had also been that drastic, but we'd seen them happen gradually, so the visual effect wasn't as stark.

The bass adapted well enough, but we worried along with everyone else. This wasn't our home, but it was a great thing in a world where great things are increasingly rare, and it seemed to be fading away. The fishing had still been okay and might have continued that way for a while to come, but this clearly couldn't have gone on indefinitely. I remembered the so-called "recovery operations" back home where fishermen were invited to come kill all the fish in the reservoirs that were being drained. There was a practical reason for it (why let all those perfectly good fish go to waste?) but it was still sort of chilling.

The fishermen still came to the Sand Hills, and they were still on vacation, so they were happy enough, but there was a new wariness in people's eyes that, even among fishermen in the effective middle of nowhere, matched the national mood.

But then the drought broke back home the winter before our last trip—or at least began to break—with above-average mountain snowpacks, spring rains and a full runoff. Northern Nebraska got its share of those storms, and of course runoff from the east slope of the Rockies flows downhill in more or less that direction until it hits the Mississippi. We didn't expect it to happen so quickly, but by the time we arrived in Nebraska in early June, most of the lakes were either back up to their former levels or close to it. Except one.

We asked Jeri about that lake a few days into the trip. She said people were catching some fish there, but the water was still real low and the hardware fishermen were having trouble with the thick weeds that usually stay down until later in the year. "It's that real stringy stuff with the tiny little white flowers," she said.

This lake had seemed to shrink more than most over the drought years, although that may have been an optical illusion caused by its small size to begin with and its gently sloping banks, where a six-inch drop in the water level could expose five or six feet of bottom. Whatever, the flooded timber where we caught many bass six and seven years ago was now thirty steps from the waterline—maybe five more steps than last year—and the lake didn't seem to be recharging after the drought along with the others.

We hiked into it and, as promised, it was choked with duckweed, with stalks like tangles of wet baling twine and mats of tiny little white flowers at the surface. But there were still strips of open water along three sides, ranging from twenty to maybe sixty or seventy feet wide, as well as some unreachable potholes out in the weed beds. Grass had sprouted around the edges on what had once been lake bottom, making the new shoreline look ominously permanent.

We split up to wade-fish from shore and I ended up on the far side of the lake, where I started seeing bass boiling in the strip of open water between me and the weeds. I checked the water the way fly fishers do and saw that it was crawling with small, pale-green damselfly nymphs. But before I changed flies, I made a few casts with my usual size-4 deer-hair diving frog and immediately got a hard strike. You have to love that about bass. Like us humans, they can be easy marks because they're always looking for something bigger and better.

The fish liked a loud plop and a few short, swimming pulls, then a rest. As soon as the bug stopped moving, they'd hit it from behind, coming up on what would be the critter's blind side. When a largemouth bass eats something the size of a frog, it opens a maw nearly as big around as its own head and takes it in a single, gulping swallow. The frog is floating quietly in the sunlight one second; swallowed whole by an unseen predator the next. A fisherman naturally loves to see this, but when you stop and think about it, it's sort of horrifying.

We fished that lake till evening and caught many bass. They were well fed and healthy and most were between, say, two and three pounds: about typical size for that lake, not counting the rare hog that turns up every once in a while. Aside from being shrunken and weed-choked, the lake seemed the same as always, right down to the herds of bullfrogs you flush into the water as you walk the shore.

There was the hope that after another wet or even just normal year, the springs would finally freshen and the lake would pump back up along with all the others, but there was no way to know short of waiting to see. The lakes around there constitute the surface water of the Oglala Aquifer (not the underground inland sea you might picture, but millions of acres of wet sand), so why one lake would be a casualty of the drought while the others were refilling was a mind-numbing mystery that could include the effects of global warming, too many deep wells, geologic wrinkles in the water table and natural weather patterns that meteorologists now say may extend over tens of thousands of years.

In the long run, you can't beat yourself up for not knowing what can't be known and it may have occurred to me then, as it does now, that there's something comic about two grown men worrying about a lake while catching bass from it hand over fist. When you're really hammering fish, you begin to feel that you really are some fisherman, but then you also can't quite shake the knowledge that with more fish crammed into a smaller lake, you have a distinct advantage.

If the lake refills again over the next few years, fine, but if it finally does dry up, there'll be no one to blame and no one to sue—and there will still be a dozen others within driving distance that are full to the brim. It will just be something that happened, proving that we're older now and remember when things were different.

I'd had the same kind of mixed feelings about Skeeter that year, too. I was happy to see him still there, while at the same time I wondered how much longer he could possibly last. He's always the first thing we look for when we pull into camp and this last time he was the first thing we saw: the familiar fuzzy white lump sitting with his back to us in the middle of the dirt road. He was deaf as a post by then, so I had to get out of the truck, walk around in front of him and politely ask him to move. When he did, I saw that his slow pace had turned into a full-blown, stiff-legged gimp. He did seem happy enough to see me though, at least in the reserved, dignified way of elderly terriers.

Skeeter was a venerable seventeen years old that year, but he was still his old self in the ways that count. We learned that earlier that year he'd stolen some venison steaks from a group of campers, buried them in a grove of junipers out back and only dug them up days later, after his victims had packed up and left. I know humans in their prime who aren't capable of that kind of restraint.

We fished the lake till dusk, when the breeze turned cool and a bank of clouds as thick as mashed potatoes piled in from the northwest, promising the kind of frog-strangling Midwestern rain I've always loved. I'm not formally religious, but I do have some ideas in that direction and one has to do with the perpetual circle water makes from rain and snow to streams and rivers to oceans to evaporation to rain and snow again. Constantly living through the last days of one thing and the first days of another can give you a chronic tickle at the back of your neck, but it helps to remember that the water we fish in now is the first and only water we've ever had.

The thunderheads were charcoal-gray on the bottom, shading to brilliant rosy pink up at 30,000 feet. There were still a few damselflies hatching, but the air had cooled and the bass had gone off, with just the odd boil here and there, mostly out of casting range. A small flock of black terns skimmed the open water looking for baitfish. A narrow shaft of late sun snuck in under the storm and painted the whole place in that sentimental gold light we all recognize from full-page ads for expensive fly rods. As near as we could figure— and it was only a guess—we had caught at least fifty bass between us. In terms of sheer numbers, it was probably the best day of bass fishing I've ever had.

We made it back to the truck just as the storm let loose

and so we ducked under the camper shell, still in our waders and with our rods still strung. This was a good, pounding downpour complete with lightning and waves of pea-sized hail. It made such a racket on the aluminum roof that it was impossible to talk, so we just sat there for a while enjoying the storm.

Chapter 18

IN MOUNTAINOUS country, streams carve canyons and trout live in streams. That's the plain logic behind the long walks fishermen take into these narrow valleys with cold water at the bottom, although you can't exactly turn your back on the scenery either. Canyons are inherently beautiful. It has something to do with stunted pines hanging on by their fingernails, all that exposed geology and a kind of other-worldliness. You're up here. The stream is way the hell down there: an impossibly distant place in plain sight, like the moon.

You can drift-fish some canyon streams in style if there's good enough access at the top and enough water to float your boat, but canyons like that are really pretty rare in the Rocky Mountains and the few we do have can get a little crowded in season. You can walk up the many smaller, less accessible canyons from the bottom, where there's often a trailhead, get-

188

ting as far in as you can in a day and staying late because the walk out will be mostly downhill. But in longer canyons with streams too skinny to float, there's that stretch in the middle you can get curious about. It's the place beyond normal day-hike range where the trails peter out; the place above where most people, including you, turn around. You can make a fair guess at what's in there, but you can't know until you've seen it for yourself.

Short of mounting the full backpacking expedition, the way you get in there is to go over the lip of the canyon some-where in the middle, thinking you might find bigger trout and fewer fishermen because the terrain will keep out the fainthearted. At least that's how you feel when you suck it up and climb into a real gnarly one, knowing that at the end of the day, after lots of hiking and wading and with your water bottles empty, you'll have to climb back out again.

It's always a toss-up. If remoteness and difficulty could so easily be translated into fish size, any fisherman in decent shape could just walk to where the big ones are, but we all know it's never that simple. Climbing into a canyon to fish is a model of the human condition in that giving in to temptation is easy because it's all downhill, but once there it may not be what you expected, and then getting back out can be a son of a bitch.

Whenever I look into an especially forbidding river gorge, I think of Cardiac Canyon on the Henry's Fork in Idaho be-cause it's one I let scare me away. According to the story, it was named for the people who'd had heart attacks trying to climb back out of it after a day of fishing. There's also the one about the guy who kept a twelve-pound rainbow that he wanted to mount, but who then dumped it on the ground halfway out because he couldn't carry it any farther.

I doubt any of that is true because it sounds too much like what you'd make up to protect a good fishing spot, being careful not to go over the top by throwing in killer grizzly bears and seven-foot rattlesnakes. Still, the last time we were on the Henry's Fork, A.K. and I decided not to hike into the canyon, but to fish some easier water upstream. I guess you could say we were among the fainthearted, and if it was all just a local fishermen's trick, it worked.

Maybe to make up for that, he and I and our friend Dave Brown climbed into a god-awful deep canyon in western Canada a few years later where we caught many large west-slope cutthroats while keeping an eye out for grizzlies—not the kind you invent to scare off the competition, but flesh-and-blood bears that leave actual tracks in the wet sand. We survived. The hike back out was a death march.

And there's that small canyon in Wyoming some friends and I fish that is, in fact, crawling with rattlesnakes. They're not seven feet long, but I could wish they were so they'd be easier to see. There's a mythology to canyon fishing that's always just true enough.

More recently, Vince and I hiked into a stream canyon on a trip to southern Wyoming. We'd fished this river several times lower down where it's wider and deeper and just big enough to float a raft early in the season. The fishing is good in that lower stretch when the flow is right and the hatches are on, and it's not half-bad even when things are a little off. If there are no bugs around, you can still usually noodle up some nice-sized trout on streamers.

We'd also hiked into it way up in the headwaters, where it's smaller and more rugged and where the fishing is just fine, but nothing to write home about. There are something like sixteen or eighteen miles of stream between those two spots, so this time we went in closer to the middle of the canyon, just to see more of a stream we'd come to like and to try to see how far up the good fishing went.

This was what I'd call a moderate canyon, the kind where the view from the top is impressive, but not breathtaking enough to make you second-guess your age and physical condition. The round-trip hike wasn't the hardest I've ever done, but as near as we can figure, we covered about nine miles with some serious ups-and-downs along the way, and when it was all over I felt like I'd done an honest day's work. As a fishing writer, I could say it *was* work, but that's a claim that doesn't fool many. Still, there are days when fishing feels like a job because it's hard and because it seems necessary, even if it's not always clear why. And anyway, it's good for a writer to have something physical to do that's away from the desk and seems important. As Larry McMurtry said, writing itself is a sedentary profession "in which one gets up in the morning and then sits right back down."

This was a hot, dry day in July and we went in light, hiking and wading in shorts with the minimum amount of gear in day packs. I carried two twenty-ounce water bottles and pre-hydrated before we started out to avoid carrying more. That's a trick Ed taught me from his firefighting days with the U.S. Forest Service and it's one of the most useful outdoor tips I've ever gotten. In the hour or so before you set out, you drink all the water you think you can hold, plus a little more: so much your stomach distends and you slosh when you walk; so much you feel you might barf. It's uncomfortable at first, but if you do it right, you can hike for hours in the heat before you get thirsty.

Of course there are always those filter bottles, but I'm

wary of them. The year before, I came home from that fishing trip to Maine with a dose of giardia that I'm convinced I got by drinking from a friend's filter bottle. I heard later that those particular bottles had been recalled because of a defect, but there's no guarantee it was the bottle in the first place. My doctor told me you can get giardia through a cut, or by splashing stream water in your eye, or by not boiling river water long enough before you brew the coffee. He said that, given the life I live, he was surprised I'd never had it before.

But intestinal parasites make a lasting impression—and I'm suspicious of technology anyway—so now, when I'm tempted to use a filter bottle, I ask myself, Is a drink of cool water worth six weeks riding the porcelain bus? So far, the answer has always been no.

We fished the canyon the way you do when you're prospecting a new place. We'd work a stretch of stream methodically, making a dozen casts to every crease and slick so as not to miss anything; then we'd cover some water more quickly, cherry-picking the best-looking spots; then we'd hike half a mile and start again. The idea wasn't so much to bear down and fish as to cover ground and see what was there.

This was a good-looking canyon. Between bare scree slopes and cliff faces there were tall spruce and pine trees with mixed aspen and river birch and shrubs like maple and alder, sometimes scattered, sometimes in thick groves and impenetrable thickets. On the insides of the widest bends there were actual forests, miniature but complete, with dark stands of mature spruce edging onto broken clearings with suckering aspens, grass, wildflowers, standing snags from old burns and tangles of deadfall from blowdowns.

Vegetation makes a canyon cooler and prettier, but it also puts all kinds of organic stuff in the stream to form the foundation of a food chain: something for bugs to eat so trout can eat the bugs so kingfishers, ospreys and river otters can eat the trout. Raw, bare rock canyons are spectacular, but they can be unfriendly to fish.

The runoff had been high that year and had lasted all the way through June, so the stream had only recently dropped to a fishable level. Vince and I had tried to fish it when we were up in that country a month earlier, but when we went to look at it at the mouth of the canyon, it was still way too high and cold. As it turned out, we fished elsewhere and did fine. Luckily, there's still plenty of public "elsewhere" in the interior West.

We went back to the same canyon almost a month later, on a bright, sunny day in July when the stream had finally dropped and cleared enough to fish. It was so hot and dry by then that when I fell in and soaked myself to the armpits, it didn't feel all that bad after the initial shock, and I dried out right down to my skin in an hour. Even in a normally wet summer like this, people from places like Pennsylvania and Oregon are amazed at the dryness here, and what some mistake for altitude sickness is often just dehydration enhanced by mild sunstroke, easily prevented with lots of water, sunscreen and a wide-brimmed straw hat.

We explored a few miles of stream through the middle of the canyon and caught trout off and on all day. I was casting a size-10 Dave's Hopper pattern—an obvious choice for a summer day with no hatch—and it brought up just enough fish to keep me from ever trying anything else. Most of the trout were browns, with one or two rainbows thrown in, and they ranged all the way from dinks just barely big enough to get a grip on the hook to relative bruisers a foot long. (Several generations of trout is the sign of a healthy, self-sustaining population.) With the bright sun and no hatch, we knew these would have been the eager trout that would bite when there was no real reason to, but then the few dumb fish that live in every stream are a fisherman's best friends.

When you live and fish in the mountains, you naturally become a student and devotee of canyons, learning about their unique ecology and working out how best to catch some of their trout. You also develop a sense of privacy about them. When you're down in a canyon you can be left alone in a profound way. Even if someone you're with is dumb enough to bring a cell phone, he'll never get a signal.

But lately I'd had to switch gears so I could think about canyons the way others sometimes do: in the cold terms of engineering, business and politics. That hadn't ruined fishing for me by a long shot—so far, nothing has ever ruined fishing—but it *had* put me into a state I hadn't quite figured out what to do with.

It had been only a few weeks since the regional water conservancy board sent notices to some of the people in the valley where I live to tell them that their homes were sitting within the footprint of one of five possible sites for a new reservoir, and that if this site were chosen, their property would be condemned. The notices were just that brief, and postcard-sized to save postage: the bare minimum notification required by law.

It took a week or so to flesh out the details after the initial panic, but eventually we learned that the "scoping meeting"—where the process of eliminating four sites and settling on one would begin—would be held in a scant two and a half months, and that's how long we had to put together whatever case we decided to make in our defense.

As it turned out, only those whose homes would actually be flooded were notified, but there'd also be a "buffer zone" around the reservoir that would eat up more properties, and if a recreation easement was added later, even more properties would be condemned. Those who'd been notified amounted to something like half the people who could lose their homes, but then that's a standard tactic of government-supported business interests. Incomplete notification and short deadlines are both ways of keeping opposition to a minimum until it's too late.

Of course a new slug of reservoirs along the Front Range was one of the things we should have seen coming when the water people launched their ad campaign the previous year, the one claiming that the drought wasn't really over, even as rivers flooded and reservoirs filled. (Actual water and the politics of water amount to parallel universes where there's invariably not enough of one and too much of the other.) This dam project was billed as drought relief, but it didn't take more than a day's worth of research to learn that the water would actually be used for new developments in seven towns in Boulder and Larimer counties. It was a typical scam of its type: a straight-ahead business deal worth millions to a handful of developers, backed by the federal Bureau of Reclamation and pitched as a public service.

When I finally got my hands on a good large-scale map of the proposed reservoir, it looked like an alien fungus growing in the canyon of our modest little stream, but then I also couldn't help but see some potential. The lower end of the reservoir would be too deep and steep-sided, so you couldn't fish Zeke's place with anything short of down-riggers, but Dry Hollow would be an interesting rocky bay and the arroyos around Suter's and Erik's houses would be narrow arms where you could cast ants, beetles and hoppers on summer afternoons.

The state Division of Wildlife would almost surely stock a reservoir like this, and even if they didn't, small, wild brown trout would dribble in from the stream above, populate the bigger water and grow fat, the same way tiny brook trout in a mountain stream will pig out in a new beaver pond.

My own place was about a quarter mile away from and a few hundred feet higher than the proposed upstream water line, not in the reservoir or the buffer zone, possibly in a recreation easement if they wanted that much of the valley. It was a position from which I could sit back to see what would happen, with a fair chance that I'd end up with a trout lake in the backyard and fewer neighbors, some of whom I'd miss.

But that was a passing thought and within days I'd joined the hastily assembled nonprofit group that was organized to fight the project, chipped in money for the inevitable lawyer and somehow ended up on the board of directors, even though in these situations I tend to be a better follower than leader. There are just times when it seems necessary to try to tip over the giant, or at least make it stumble enough to momentarily lose its place.

I have to say this was one of my best experiences along those lines. For one thing, I met some neighbors I didn't know. I suppose we seem like a standoffish bunch up here, but I prefer to think that we all moved up a dead-end valley in order to be left alone and we're courteous enough to return the favor.

Almost everyone involved was what you'd call middle-aged, and although to most outward appearances some had gone straight, we were still children of the 1960s who'd learned early on about the politics of resistance and had since developed a layman's working knowledge of bureaucracy. A few journalistic types also brought to the table an understanding of how to manipulate the media, which can be embarrassingly easy at times.

We made a few stabs at political support, but we did it halfheartedly and without much hope. It's always hard to know which way to go with politicians because, as they say here in the West, the Democrats want your guns and the Republicans want your land, so you're pretty much on your own. I did get the opportunity to yell at and then storm out on our county commissioner, which I found to be deeply satisfying after I'd calmed down.

Of course it wasn't all idealism and solidarity. We had our share of hysterics and loose cannons, and at one meeting a friend and neighbor whispered to me, "You know, there are some people here I wouldn't mind *seeing* underwater." Some personal spats naturally developed, the kind that will be played out for years to come in the ways you'd expect from a small, scattered community that's been described as "part Mayberry and part *Northern Exposure.*"

But in general we were well organized, thorough, businesslike and relentless, right down to the lawyer we hired. We interviewed two attorneys, one of whom was a young, idealistic environmentalist and a real nice guy, but we ended up hiring the slick, ruthless one because who wants a nice guy for a lawyer? That sort of thing.

I went through the usual emotional stages these things always elicit: disbelief, despondency, cynicism, anger bordering on hatred and finally a kind of murderous caginess. You'd think that after doing this dozens of times over the years I could go right to the end and save myself the turmoil, but apparently it's all necessary as a sort of ritualistic process of elimination.

Of course the New Agers would like to do away with anger entirely, but they can't because it's in the genes and because it's a useful emotion that makes you act when you might otherwise just sit there pouting. Anger is what separates a cool customer from a cold fish, an adversary from a victim.

Because of my limited talents, I was put in charge of researching species diversity in the valley. I managed most of that with the help of a friendly librarian at the Division of Wildlife Research Library in Fort Collins. (If you ever wake up one morning trying to think of a reason not to shoot yourself, just think of helpful librarians.)

I won't reproduce my entire report here (as tempting as that is), but the valley in general and the stream canyon in particular are home to no fewer than seventy species of birds, several dozen large and small mammals (from mice and shrews to elk and mountain lion), assorted snakes, lizards and amphibians, a few small trout and forage fish and a wild diversity of foothills, high plains and riparian plant life. Among them are three threatened species and one endangered species. The last is a little plant called a Bell's twin-pod that's so unassuming you'd step on one without a second thought. It's one of those delightful little things—like the legendary snail darter—that give dam builders nightmares.

Others found that there are something like twenty American Indian archeological sites here, as well as geological features and habitat types unusual enough to be officially recognized by county agencies, and a geologic fault near the proposed dam site that could make it unsafe.

The lawyer said it all made a good, voluminous case, and if

nothing else we could bury the bastards in documentation, all of which, by law, would have to go into their own report and then be examined in the environmental impact statement.

Anyway, all the information we'd gathered had gone to the attorney and then on to paid consultants who would understand what it meant and how best to present it. In the end, it would make a case that could prevail on its own merits or, more likely, make our own little canyon look like more trouble than it was worth: a strange way to think of a place you've come to love and call home, but necessary under the circumstances. There would be more to do, but in the temporary lull it occurred to me that when trying to keep life simple becomes a full-time job, something has gone horribly wrong. That's when Vince and I went back to fish that canyon in Wyoming.

By late afternoon, we were as far up the canyon as we were going to get, sitting side by side on a flat rock in front of the ruin of an old miner's cabin. It was mostly collapsed, but you could tell there'd been one roughly eight-by-ten-foot log room custom-made to fit the only available flat spot. Around the side was a hand-dug glory hole with the spoil sloping down to the creek. The view from what was left of the front door was magnificent.

It's easy to get romantic about old cabins and I caught myself hoping that the guy loved his solitude and found some gold, but I also know there's more misery than we'd like to think in the history of these mountains, so it's just as likely he was desperate and half crazy from loneliness. Maybe he at least caught some trout for supper in the evenings. That made a pretty picture, although a hardscrabble miner just out for some fish would probably choose a quarter stick of dynamite instead of a dry fly.

It was late enough in the day that although the lip of the canyon was still in bright sun, the stream had been swallowed in shade and the air had turned cool. Through the heat of the day I'd emptied my water bottles and I was thirsty again. Vince was drinking from a filter bottle that he'd filled at the stream, but my unreasoning fear of gut bugs made it easier to say "No thanks" when he offered it.

We could have stayed till evening, hoping to catch the hour or so of furious fishing that streams like this can hand out right before nightfall, but that would have meant groping four and a half miles in the dark to get out, most of it steeply up-hill on nothing wider than a game trail: a good way to break either an ankle or a fly rod.

And anyway, we'd learned what we came to find out. On a hot, bright day with no hatches, we'd caught a fair number of trout up to a foot long, and there'd been those two big ones. Vince said he was playing a small brown when a large shape flashed it, reminding him of the enormous bull trout in British Columbia that will now and then eat a foot-long cut-throat right off your hook.

And there was the big one I missed on the grasshopper at the head of a deep, shady run; the one that splashed like a dropped anvil when he felt the hook. Really. To get that much noise and spray out of even a sixteen-inch trout, you'd have had to drop him from twenty feet. These are the hints that tell you either there's more here than you thought or your mind is playing tricks on you again, with the truth usually lying somewhere in between. So I guess we'd satisfied our curiosity as well as fishermen are ever able to do—and in the right hands, that's all fishing is: curiosity running harmlessly amok.

I'd easily fallen into the thoughtless rhythm of hiking and fishing, but when we stopped to rest, I began to think about dams and lawyers again and a little bit of the anger resurfaced, like something I'd tried to swallow but that had lodged halfway down. Sitting there on that rock, I physically shook the idea out of my head. Vince probably thought I was being pestered by a deer fly and in fact the two sensations are similar.

I said, "Well?"

Vince said, "Yeah, I guess so," and we started back.

Chapter 19

IFOUND MYSELF driving down the Thompson River Canyon on a cold, sunny afternoon just before a snow-storm; puttering along slowly, as fishermen do beside rivers so they can look at the water. Of course non-fishermen drive like bats out of hell up and down this twisty two-lane road, so every few minutes an enormous SUV would roar up from behind and tailgate me. People who do that want you to speed up, so naturally I slow down even more. I know that's a dangerously passive-aggressive maneuver—provoking road rage without actually engaging in it—but I enjoy watching their faces turn purple in the rear-view mirror.

Whenever I came to a gravel turnout, I'd pull over to get out and look at the river, incidentally letting a line of cars pass and ignoring the dirty looks. The water was low and clear, the air chilly, the sun bright. A breeze was coming upstream so gently you wouldn't even notice it on a warmer day, but that afternoon it was enough to cancel the effect of the sun. A big snow was in the forecast for that night or the next morning—they weren't sure which—and if the weatherman was right, the barometer would already be falling. I'm one of those who believe that approaching low-pressure fronts bring on insect hatches and make trout want to feed, although I couldn't tell you why.

Sure enough, there were some midges coming off and some trout were rising here and there. I'd park and walk up and down the shoulder of the road, staying high for the best angle, studying eddies, side channels and the foamy edges of the main current. The rises were so quiet they barely made a ring, so it was often easier to spot the fish themselves in the low, clear water. There'd be a dull flash or a moving shadow that would then materialize into a trout when you focused on it. When he'd rise—once you knew where he was—you could see the tiny half-moon-shaped crease as his nose barely broke the surface, but it would dissolve in the current before it could spread, just one more little ripple in a river full of ripples. I'd locate a few trout, then walk back to the idling pickup and drive on, almost satisfied.

I was in one of those nonpredatory moods that can settle on a fisherman late in the season. I had a fly rod with me so I had technically gone fishing, but so far I was just driving, looking at water and enjoying the relative peace and quiet. It was an ordinary weekday afternoon in late fall with not much traffic on the road, but still more than you'd think, and walking the narrow shoulder to spot fish, I'd always turn and watch at the sound of an approaching car. People drive these canyon roads the way they see cars driven in TV commercials (except these are not "professional drivers on closed courses") and they're often in less than full control of their vehicles, what with a cup of cappuccino in one hand and a cell phone in the other.

It's that familiar feeling of trying to go about your own business at your own pace while getting out of the way as annoying and dangerous things pass by too quickly, but you always look because if you're going to have to dive for your life, you want all the warning you can get.

Still, this was what you'd have to call a quiet time of year. In summer, there are five times more cars and they're usually joined by bicyclists in Spandex looking like swarms of brightly colored, poisonous insects that can descend on you suddenly and silently. And the tourist town at the head of the canyon is fully geared up in the regulation cowboy hat and rubber-tomahawk style, trying to make a year's nut in five months and then stretching it to six with Oktoberfest. It's harder work than it seems, and by midseason, the clerks in the shops have become fried from the constant pretense of hospitality. Their smiles still say "howdy," but their eyes say, "Aw, Christ, not another one."

Some tourists seem equally dazed, and not entirely by the 14,000-foot peaks looming above town or the bull elk that graze on the golf course. They seem to have realized what they probably suspected all along: that a sign saying "Come See the Real West" means this is one place where the real West no longer exists. Signs in the real West say "No Trespassing."

Still, it all works in a left-handed sort of way: The town pretends to entertain us, we pretend to be entertained, and a regional economy survives. The vague sense of insufficiency we're left with is nothing new to most Americans. In fact, it has shaped our national character. It's what makes some of us drive too fast and others just want to go fishing.

Through the summer, the river below town gets about as

crowded as you'd expect under the circumstances, that is, not too bad one day and so hideously mobbed the next that you immediately drive to one of the little creeks in the neighborhood where you can fish for smaller trout by yourself.

But by late in the year things have wound down and no one seems a bit sorry. In fact, I've long suspected that the eighty-mile-an-hour chinook winds we sometimes get at this time of year are actually a collective sigh of relief from the summer tourist industry. There are still plenty of fishermen on the river while the weather holds, but now they're mostly locals and a few day-trippers who know this little tailwater stays open longer than the other streams in the neighborhood. That afternoon there were fly casters working all the obvious, well-known pools, so I was checking out the pocket water in between. There was a lot of it, people were ignoring it, and—I hesitate to say in print—there were trout rising all over the place.

On my third or fourth stop I checked the wide tailout of a plunge pool and spotted some spawning browns. I just caught a flash out of the corner of my eye through some bare willows and then crept to a good vantage point where I could peer through the branches. The female was hovering over the redd in a few inches of water and the male was flirting desperately. It was really too late in the year for spawning at that altitude and he seemed to know that. Both fish looked to be at least twenty inches long, but then in a stream where the average trout isn't much more than a foot, it's easy to exaggerate.

What drew my attention to them was the male chasing away a smaller brown that would have been about sixteen inches, assuming the other two were as big as I thought. He did it twice in a few minutes. The smaller fish was persistent, the big male was irritated and I figured he'd hit a size-4 Muddler Minnow if I swam one in front of him. I worked out where to cross the river so as not to spook the fish and saw where I'd have to stand to get a good swing. Then I got back in the truck and drove away. I don't fish for spawners anymore; haven't for years. It's legal here in Colorado, but it still seems unfair.

This had turned out to be a surprisingly normal late summer and fall, considering that I spent most of it on the board of the organization trying to stop the proposed reservoir in our valley. That was a necessary chore, even though it took several big bites out of the fishing season, but then that's mostly my fault, since I'm unable to do two things at once without screwing up both of them.

Anyway, because of that I'd stayed near home for the most part, taking day trips to fish in two local counties, longer road trips to parts of Colorado, Wyoming and Idaho and missing roughly as many days of fishing as I did meetings, which seemed only fair.

Vince Zounek and Mike Price drove on some of those trips, but I still managed to put another 14,000 miles on my old Nissan pickup and finally just about wore it out. After back-to-back bass-fishing trips to Oklahoma and Nebraska— almost 3,000 miles in all, half of it towing a boat—the truck's master clutch cylinder blew out twenty feet from my back door. This is the kind of luck you appreciate, but don't dare count on. When I went to pick up the truck from my mechanic, I asked him what had been wrong with the part. He looked at me incredulously and said, "It was sixteen years old, man."

When the odometer climbed past 230,000 miles later in

the season, I started shopping for a newer used truck and had the usual pangs of conscience men experience over their old pickups. It was the same feeling you'd get if one day you looked at the woman you'd lived with for the last fifteen years and seriously thought, Maybe I should get a newer model with lower mileage. But regardless of what we'd been through together, this was just a car, and life does go on.

Between fishing trips and writing jobs, I'd worked with the board and incidentally learned more about the natural and cultural history of the valley in a few months than I'd uncovered on my own in six years of exploring and talking to old-timers. Aside from the fact that we didn't want to be thrown out of our homes, the valley revealed itself as a place that really shouldn't be ruined to further an economy based on replacing elk and peregrine falcons with suburbs. But of course the water board was unashamedly in the business of doing just that. It was environmental politics as usual, where each side arrives with its own assumptions and proceeds to play by its own rules, so that the result is a kind of puzzled standoff.

After the three-year drought, it had been a gloriously normal water year. Old-timers say the snowpack is about right when you can still see snow in the crack on the east face of Long's Peak on the Fourth of July. That year the crack was still white until a few days short of August.

It was also an average fire season. Forests are supposed to burn in order to stay healthy and they all do eventually, but that summer a more or less normal 18,000 acres went up, as opposed to the 620,000 acres the year before. The Overland Fire did blow by eight miles to the south, burning away from my house by ninety degrees, but then I don't remember too many years out here when I haven't seen smoke on the horizon in one direction or another.

The poor old South Platte River had also held up okay after the drought, the Hayman Fire and the flash floods the following spring. A Division of Wildlife survey done late in the year showed that although fish had been lost lower down to high summer water temperatures the year before, the only real effect in the upper river was the loss of a single age-class of trout: the youngest and smallest. That would cause a dip in fish size in years to come, but for now, the trout had survived.

The signature Blue-Winged Olive mayfly hatch came off on schedule in the fall and lasted into December, so the bugs seemed to be doing okay, too. There was no official word on whirling disease, but one biologist did say he thought the parasite had "about run its course" on the river. When I asked him if he'd care to clarify that, he said, "No, I really wouldn't."

Naturally, the upper reaches of Cheesman Canyon remained the delicious mystery they've always been. I've been told that the Division of Wildlife has only one survey station down at the bottom of the canyon, where they can hump in their electroshocking equipment without breaking their backs, so whatever is known about the upper canyon is known only to fishermen and is therefore unreliable.

Most of the high-country streams in the region didn't come down enough to fly-fish until July, but when they did come down, they fished beautifully and for some reason we spent more than the usual amount of the season exploring new local waters: the ones you can drive to and fish in a day and still get home to sleep in your own bed. If you're willing to leave early and pull back in well after midnight, that covers enough territory to last a lifetime.

On a tip from the fly-fishing mechanic who works on my truck, Vince and I found some surprisingly good-sized grayling in a tiny, uninteresting-looking creek at 11,000 feet up near the Wyoming border. On the same drainage a few weeks later, also on a tip, A.K. and I hiked up a tributary creek past the brookies and brown trout to the cutthroat water above. It took us the better part of a long summer day. We saw one hiker with a friendly black Lab, but no other fishermen. This was yet another canyon stretching twenty miles or so with access only at the top and bottom, leaving a big, rough chunk in the middle that will eventually have to be explored.

And so on. As I said, it was a surprisingly normal year.

Temperatures and rainfall that summer were about what you could reasonably expect for the region, but people stayed nervous and some of the bigger newspapers published detailed articles about whether or not the drought was really over. As you'd expect, some experts said yes, others said no, a few said maybe and a few others said that since in this climate both droughts and floods were perfectly normal, the question was moot.

The *New York Times* probably said it best: Tree ring studies indicate that periodic dry spells have been common in the West for at least the last thousand years and that the twentieth century was unusually wet. Since most of the region's water laws evolved over that last hundred years, they said, the modern settlement of the West "may have been based on a colossal miscalculation."

The water providers' request for that open-ended two billion dollars for unspecified water projects became Referendum A on the state ballot in November and was voted down two to one. Maybe people saw through the hype or maybe they just realized that it would be their money. People are more cynical now, and that's a shame, but it does make them harder to fool.

The week the scoping meeting for the dam was held, I was

on the Salmon River in Idaho fishing for fall steelhead with a small gang of friends. It was one of those big public meetings where everyone gets up to speak and I thought that was best left to cooler heads. And anyway, the fishing trip was already scheduled, so it was go then or not at all.

I'm told the meeting went well. There were TV cameras from several local stations, always a good sign for the opposition. Homeowners spoke and there were a few tears, which play well on the evening news. Our consultants presented their reports and then the lawyer summed it all up and drove the last nail by handing over a stack of documentation big enough to make even a bureaucrat swallow hard. Of course that last part might just be my own imagination, since paperwork alternately bores and terrifies me. Anyway, I was sorry I'd missed it, but only in theory.

The fishing on the Salmon River was a little slow that week, but it was the first time I caught steelhead on flies I'd tied myself, which is the kind of small milestone any fisherman will appreciate. And then one night in camp Mike Price told me my Spey-casting had gotten "pretty." He's a famous wisecracker, so I made a wisecrack myself to beat him to the punch, but for once he wasn't setting me up. It was an actual compliment.

I didn't plan on it, but it's beginning to look as though steelheading is my next thing. It's a difficult, sometimes heartbreaking, sometimes physically demanding, occasionally satisfying sport that's best taken up in your twenties or thirties instead of when you're pushing sixty, but then we're not always in control of these things. They seem to happen by themselves while we just go along for the ride, doing the best we can.

• • •

The dam project hadn't exactly fizzled, but it was at least looking somewhat promising for our side. Officially, all five sites were still up for grabs, but a source on the water board said, off the record, that our valley would likely be dropped from consideration eventually because we'd thrown up too many roadblocks. I decided to take that as a left-handed compliment.

We also learned that the board was quietly buying up land at one of the other reservoir sites to the north. (They didn't advertise it, but the transactions were in the public record.) That site was in yet another valley that was surely as unique and valuable as ours, but that lacked the constituency to hire the lawyers and go to the meetings. If the project went that way, at least no one would be evicted from their home, but it would amount to the same dam in someone else's backyard and there'd be plenty of time to feel guilty about that. Still, it was hopeful news, although officially they were still "keeping all the options open," as bureaucrats like to say.

But by then it had become obvious that although we might well skate this time, those options would *always* be open. Once the pretty little valley where you live has been identified as a good reservoir site, the dam builders are unlikely to forget about it and you're in a plodding race between big money and the eventual enlightenment of the culture.

But then recent history has taught us what fishermen have always known: that if you can't learn to live with uncertainty, you probably can't learn to live at all. Meanwhile, it was late in the season, but the trout were still biting, and I found that like any good twenty-first-century American, I could be happy enough without knowing exactly what comes next.

I'd been driving along the Thompson for a couple of hours

when I finally decided to fish a good-looking run several miles downstream. I had almost reached the point where I could have scouted rising trout all afternoon, grabbed a cup of coffee in town and driven home without ever stringing up the rod, but then something clicked. I was probably putting off fishing because I could see how hard it was going to be. Then it would have occurred to me that driving around looking at water was for dilettantes, while the real fisherman (whatever that is) would stand up and take his lumps like John Wayne. I don't actually remember thinking any of that, but it's how the process works.

I found two trout rising casually in the tail of a little slick and waded in downstream to see what was on the water. Looking upstream against the low sun, I could see scattered small flies in the air, but I had to watch a current seam for several minutes before a bug floated by. It was a midge fly about as small as they get: not much more than a speck with wings. I had some flies like that on size-26 hooks, so I lengthened my leader out to a 7x tippet and tied one on.

I must have spooked the fish in the tail of the slick because after two casts he stopped rising and hadn't started again after five minutes. Then I got a few good drifts over the fish ahead of him, but missed him when he took the fly.

A little farther upstream there were four or five trout lying in a shallow bankside slick, noodling around lazily and rising every now and then. The sun was quartering off my left shoulder and I could see them clearly, but I stayed in the shade of some ponderosa pines, crouched low and got surprisingly close without spooking them.

The first trout I got a good drift over ignored the dry fly, so I switched to a small pupa pattern I like. He ate that confidently and I somehow managed to pull him off the back of the pod and play him out downstream without spooking the rest of the fish. I rested the spot for a few minutes, then went back and hooked another trout that jumped and blew up the pool. By the time I had him landed and released, the rest of the fish were long gone.

By then the sun was off the water. There were no more bugs that I could see, and no more rises in the next hundred yards of river. I'd just caught the end of the hatch, but I'd gotten two trout, both rainbows, one about twelve inches, the other more like fourteen. Two is a good number. One fish can be a fluke, but two seems to mean that you figured it out. And once you figure it out, the game can be over if you want it to be.

The sun was almost down and the wind had picked up and turned from chilly to bitter, as it does before a front. It was blowing upslope and that often means heavy snow—maybe the first good storm of another wet winter. Now and then I could see a car whiz past on the road, but by this time the next day, driving this canyon at anything over twelve miles an hour could amount to suicide.

Suddenly that cup of coffee I'd been thinking about a few hours before started to sound really good, and getting it wouldn't be a chore in the off-season. There'd be plenty of room to park at the coffee shop and I wouldn't have to stand in line. The woman behind the counter would probably smile genuinely and might even ask how the fishing was. (The locals can always spot you for a fisherman.)

I derigged and drove the five miles up the canyon to town at a pretty good clip, keeping up with traffic for once.

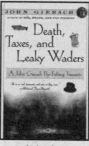

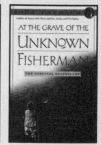